Invasion! Rome Against the Cimbri, 113–101 BC

Invasion! Rome Against the Cimbri, 113–101 BC

Philip Matyszak

Pen & Sword
MILITARY

First published in Great Britain in 2022 by
Pen & Sword Military
An imprint of
Pen & Sword Books Ltd
Yorkshire – Philadelphia

ISBN 978 1 39909 731 4

A CIP catalogue record for this book is available from the British Library.

Typeset by Mac Style
Printed in the UK by CPI Group (UK) Ltd, Croydon, CR0 4YY.

Pen & Sword Books Limited incorporates the imprints of Atlas, Archaeology, Aviation, Discovery, Family History, Fiction, History, Maritime, Military, Military Classics, Politics, Select, Transport, True Crime, Air World, Frontline Publishing, Leo Cooper, Remember When, Seaforth Publishing, The Praetorian Press, Wharncliffe Local History, Wharncliffe Transport, Wharncliffe True Crime and White Owl.

For a complete list of Pen & Sword titles please contact

PEN & SWORD BOOKS LIMITED
47 Church Street, Barnsley, South Yorkshire, S70 2AS, England
E-mail: enquiries@pen-and-sword.co.uk
Website: www.pen-and-sword.co.uk

Or

PEN AND SWORD BOOKS
1950 Lawrence Rd, Havertown, PA 19083, USA
E-mail: Uspen-and-sword@casematepublishers.com
Website: www.penandswordbooks.com

Contents

Introduction

For a century after the Hannibalic War, Rome went through a turbulent period of savage politics and almost unrelenting warfare. Yet only once in all that time was Rome fighting for its very survival. For the most part Rome fought wars of conquest, as what was once a small city in Latium grew unstoppably into an empire which spanned the Mediterranean world. In the second century BC, Rome fought the heirs of Alexander the Great, conquering Macedon and humbling the mighty Seleucid empire. It was not enough that after the Hannibalic war Rome had eliminated Carthage as a rival power in the western Mediterranean – at the insistence of Cato the Elder and his supporters, Carthage was wiped out altogether in 146 BC.

Yet, for all that Rome seemed to be growing ever more powerful, all was not well within the Republic. Almost throughout the history of Rome, there had been tension between the aristocratic upper class and the working people who powered the Roman economy and supplied recruits for the army. Generally, these class disputes were solved with minimal violence, but after the Carthaginian wars these disputes became violent and bloody. In part this was because the balance of power had swung firmly in favour of the aristocracy, and attempts to redress that issue by reformers such as the Gracchus brothers were met with violent repression that led to the deaths of both Gracchi and many of their followers.

This repression coarsened the political process but also damaged Rome's military ability. Roman commanders had previously been selected at least partly on merit, but the aristocratic capture of Rome's political institutions meant that generalship and actual military ability became increasingly separate qualities. Romans of noble family who should not have been put in charge of a toy gladiator set commanded armies which they saw only as tools by which they could gain profit from loot and political kudos. Towards the end of the second century this had led to a series of unnecessary defeats in Spain and elsewhere, but none of these defeats threatened Rome seriously enough to necessitate a change in the status quo. All that changed with the arrival of the Cimbri. The Cimbri not only threatened Rome – they threatened to destroy it altogether.

The story of the Cimbri is both fascinating and frustrating. These people were every bit as much a threat to Rome as Hannibal had been in the previous century. Yet, while everyone with even a vague interest in Roman history has heard of Hannibal and Rome's wars with Carthage, very few people other than professional historians have heard of the Cimbri. Yet here we see a tribe from the location of modern Denmark leave their traditional home and begin a massive southward trek. This was no relatively trivial group such as the 30,000 or so Visigoths who captured and sacked Rome in AD 410. The Cimbric invasion of half a millennium previously was literally ten times larger – and that is before we count Cimbric allies such as the Teutones and Ambrones who are said to have doubled the size of the invading host. In numbers alone the Cimbri were a terrifying menace.

The reasons why the Cimbri suddenly decided to leave their northern homeland are controversial and discussed at length in the opening chapters of this book. Once they had left Jutland, the Cimbri moved slowly south in search of a new home, including Illyria and Spain in their travels. During the course of those travels they met Roman army after Roman army and – at least partly due to poor generalship on the Roman side – crushed each of these in turn. One such battle was among the greatest Roman defeats ever recorded, a massacre of the legions comparable with that at Cannae in 216 BC. Yet, while Cannae is known to every military historian, few remember the 80,000 or so Romans whom the Cimbri killed at Arausio in 105 BC.

Had the Cimbri followed up their success at Arausio with a march on Rome, it is quite possible that this book would be written in a very different language. Rome's Italian allies had very little fondness for the corrupt and oppressive state which governed them (they were to rise in a concerted rebellion against Rome just over a decade later). Had the Cimbri taken Rome, it is quite possible that the Italians might have joined the Cimbri in stamping out the last remnants of that failing state. Rome's nascent empire would have collapsed and later histories would talk of Rome as they talk of the Seleucid and Neo-Babylonian empires, states which briefly expanded to occupy huge swathes of territory only to quickly collapse once again.

So, given that the Cimbric wars brought Rome to the brink of extinction and involved hundreds of thousands of men on both sides, how is it that so few know of the Cimbri today?

Probably the main reason why the story of the Cimbric migration has been largely forgotten is because few tellings of that story from antiquity have survived the vagaries of time. We know a great deal of a relatively trivial war fought just before the Cimbric invasion because a detailed history of that war has come down to us. This is Sallust's account of the Jugurthine War, fought in Africa against the renegade Numidian king Jugurtha. As a writer, Sallust is capable of punchy prose and he held little back in his ferocious condemnation of the corrupt oligarchy which dominated contemporary Roman politics. His is a very readable text, and for that reason it has survived the passing millennia.

As a result we have some quite detailed accounts of skirmishes in desert sandpits which involved a few hundred men on either side. Meanwhile north of the Alps, armies of tens of thousands clashed in battles the date and location of which are now mostly a matter of conjecture. We are ignorant of so many of the key details of the Cimbric wars that it is hard to pay much attention to what remains. So, while the Jugurthine War in Africa features prominently in accounts of the later Republic, the much more important Cimbric wars tend to merit only a quick paragraph or two.

It is not that these wars were considered unimportant at the time. Two of the generals involved – Lutatius Catulus and Cornelius Sulla – wrote detailed campaign notes in the style later improved upon by Julius Caesar when he described his conquest of Gaul. The historian Livy wrote a history of Rome from the founding to his own time, and in this he gave considerable space to the Cimbric wars (as we know from the surviving skimpy summaries of his lost chapters). A later historian, Appian of Alexandria, dedicated several of the early chapters of his *Gallic Wars* to the Cimbric invasion.

One of the most important players in the final stages of the Cimbric invasion was the Roman general Caius Marius. Marius was also the general who brought the Jugurthine War to an end, a key player in the Roman civil war of 83–81 BC, and an important figure in Roman politics for much of his adult life. Yet his biographer, Plutarch, dedicates fully a third of his *Life of Marius* to the events of the Cimbric wars. They were that important.

Yet, of all the texts mentioned above, only Plutarch has come down to the modern era. Of Appian's *Gallic Wars* barely a few pathetic summaries remain while the military histories of Sulla and Catulus may survive,but only as vague echoes in the text of Plutarch, who probably used them as a source. From a modern perspective it would have been much better if Livy had not written about the Cimbric wars at all, because all of the later chapters of his epic history are now lost. However, Livy's history and these now lost chapters were around in the early Empire, and because Livy had done such an excellent job of describing the Cimbric war, few others felt up to the task of writing something else as good. So we have not only lost one of our best sources of the war, but few inferior sources ever existed.

The Cimbric wars are not the only victim of the textual lacuna which exists in our supply of reliable sources in Roman historiography from the end of the Macedonian wars to the start of the Roman civil wars, but they are one of the most frustrating. To fill the gaps in our knowledge modern historians have had to scrabble through passing comments and casual asides in later works and to rely on ancient historians such as Florus and Orosius, who not only had some rather severe biases which have to be allowed for but also wrote some four centuries after the events they were describing.

As a result Florus and Orosius provide, for example, almost totally different accounts for the decisive battle of Vercellae. About the only thing these two historians are agreed upon is that the battle did actually happen – somewhere. Incredible to relate, the location is lost of one of the most crucial battles in the history of the Roman Republic, a battle which might have destroyed Rome had the legions gone down in defeat as they had done just a few years previously at Arausio.

Nevertheless, the Cimbric wars are just too important to ignore altogether, and in recent years it has become easier to put together a more complete picture of what actually happened. This is partly due to some excellent work by Danish archaeologists who have slowly assembled a more complete picture of who the Cimbri were (even their ethnicity is controversial) and what happened to the tribe both before their massive migration and after the survivors straggled home.

There have also been some excellent modern studies which have looked particularly at the latter stages of the wars. Here we at least have the framework of Plutarch's *Life of Marius* with which to work. Plutarch was a biographer and a priest of Apollo who seldom left his native town of Charonea in Greece. Plutarch does not pretend to be a military historian and it is doubtful that he ever saw a *pilum* thrown in anger. Therefore, when describing the life of Marius from the perspective of a philosopher and a moralist Plutarch does an excellent job of critiquing the ethical deficiencies in Marius' character. However, he is considerably more shaky when it comes to cohort deployments and unit numbers – which, to be fair, did not greatly interest him anyway.

However, Plutarch was an excellent researcher and he made good use of his sources, so by and large our issues with Plutarch are with what he does not choose to tell us, and his (mis)interpretation of the military events he is attempting to describe. He is relatively solid on the actual facts that he does give. Therefore, by combining Plutarch with other less-helpful sources, a credible reconstruction of the later phases of the war has become possible.

Another reason for attempting such a reconstruction is because the geography of northern Italy puts a tactical straitjacket on any invader coming across the Alps. Once Plutarch has given the names of a few key locations it becomes possible to discover which routes must have been taken by the generals on either side and which incidents could only have occurred at certain points. As a result, we can follow the Teutones as these allies of the Cimbri made their way towards the Piedmontese Alps, and do so with a fair degree of accuracy. Likewise it is possible to reconstruct with some certainty the careful manoeuvres of Catulus as he struggled to keep his demoralized army intact in the face of difficult odds and lose-lose tactical choices.

What is missing – and probably never existed – is the other side of the story. The Roman writers present the Cimbri as almost a blind force of nature, capricious and hugely destructive. No accounts exist to tell us of what the Cimbri thought they were doing, of the councils that informed their fateful decisions or how the Cimbri themselves thought of their epic migration. Even with only the scattered textual evidence which exists for the period it is reasonably clear what was happening in Roman politics at this point (not least because Plutarch understood politics a lot better than he understood military tactics). Why the Romans chose the generals they did is reasonably clear, as is what the Roman people thought about it all. For the Cimbric side nothing exists but conjecture.

This leads to another important consideration. Because all the accounts of the Cimbric wars are from Roman sources it is natural to think of the Romans as the 'good guys', because that is how the Romans thought of themselves. After all, defending one's homeland against an invading horde is what the good guys do, right? Yet, if that is the case, one must consider the morality of the Romans who had in recent years been the invading horde attacking Greece, Macedonia, Spain, Sicily and Africa, among other places. The Romans were hardly in a position to claim that attacking and conquering other peoples was a bad thing, and by and large they do not. It is a modern demand that all stories have a moral element and pit heroes against villains; the Romans did not think that way and when considering the Cimbric wars we should not either.

In much the same way, the term 'barbarian' is used in this text not as a pejorative but as the Romans themselves used it. That is, as a catch-all term to describe the Germans, Celts, Illyrians, Thracians and other peoples who lived beyond the northern extent of Roman power. (And without going into the modern ethnographic debate as to who the 'Celts' were, that term is also used here in the Roman sense – basically people of northwest Europe who were not German.) It is also worth noting that if the term 'barbaric' is to be used as a pejorative, the Romans themselves were pretty barbaric. They had demonstrated that in the previous generation by conquering and looting the historic city of Corinth in Greece at the same time as they were destroying the city and culture of Carthage, basically because they could.

Nor were the Romans of this time western civilization's dauntless defenders against the barbarian horde. At this time in the history of the Roman Republic, the fall of Rome would not have been followed by the fall of civilization in Italy, let alone elsewhere. Outside Italy civilization was doing just fine in the Hellenic kingdoms of Seleucia and Ptolemaic Egypt, and also in the cities of the Greek diaspora scattered around the western Mediterranean. In Italy itself civilization was well-entrenched in places where the Cimbri could neither easily reach nor particularly wanted to, such as Etruria, Naples and Tarentum. Even in the barbarian north-west urbanization, trade and economic development were proceeding apace in Gaul and Britain well before the later, dramatic Roman intervention. And that is before we mention the already ancient cultures of Judea, Mesopotamia and points east. In fact it is arguable that western civilization might have progressed further and better if Roman power had not expanded to encompass the whole of it and taken it all down together when the later Empire finally fell.

So, given the roles and character of the opposing sides, the Cimbric wars should not be seen as a morality tale of good versus evil, especially when one considers that in all of Roman politics at this point only one character – Rutilius Rufus – really comes across as a decent human being. (And he was condemned and exiled for precisely that reason.)

There are other and better reasons for studying the Cimbric wars. These wars helped to transform Roman politics and greatly assisted the rise of the *populares* – the democratic (or demagogic, depending on one's viewpoint) approach to politics ultimately taken up by Julius Caesar. We also see in the Cimbric wars the rise of the rivalry between Sulla and Marius, which led to the first of the great civil wars that tore apart and destroyed the Roman Republic.

Furthermore, the Cimbric wars demonstrate Rome's famous adaptability in action as the state struggled to cope with manpower shortages and the need to drastically change its military practices to adapt to the existential threat posed by the invaders. The army which emerged from the Cimbric wars was the army which Caesar used to conquer Gaul, which Pompey used to conquer the Levant and which Augustus used to capture Egypt. It was the army which won an empire for Rome.

All of the above are good reasons for studying the Cimbric wars. Yet there is another and possibly better reason for doing so, the reason why Livy, Appian and Plutarch told the tale in the first place – because it is a cracking good story which deserves to be re-told for that reason alone.

A note on translations: All the quotes from ancient sources have been translated by the author from the original language versions available from the Perseus Archive at www.perseus.tufts.edu

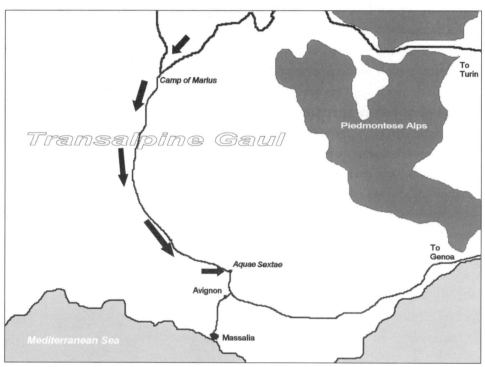

Sketch showing a suggested route of the Teutones to the Battle of Aquae Sextae.

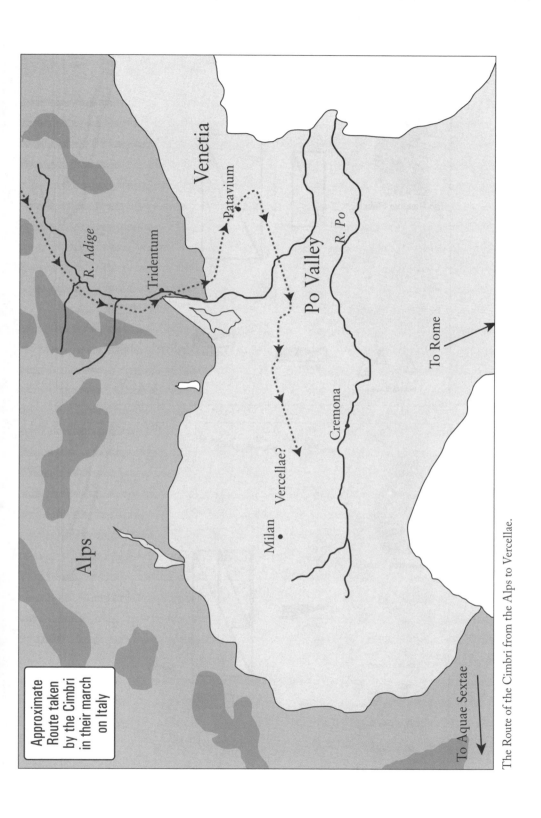

The Route of the Cimbri from the Alps to Vercellae.

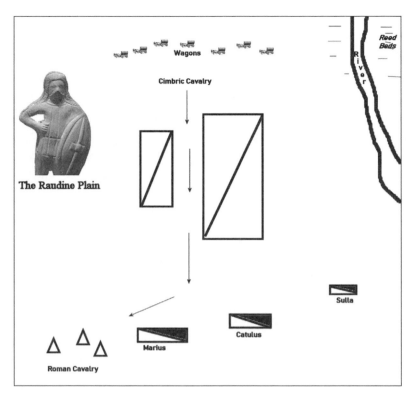

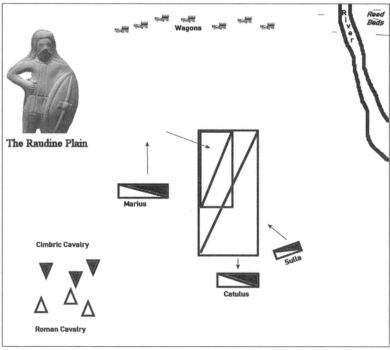

A reconstruction of the Battle of Vercellae.

Chapter 1

Who Were the Cimbri?

Over 2,300 years ago, a scientific expedition set out to explore the unknown. The explorers were led by a Greek called Pytheas, an astronomer and geographer from what is now Marseilles in France. One objective of the expedition was to find the famed land of the Hyperboreans, where the ice never melted and the sun shone even at midnight. It goes without saying that after his expedition to the north Pytheas was able to confirm that the midnight sun and unmelting ice were not fantastic stories but literally the cold, hard truth. Yet this expedition is of further significance, because it represents the first time that peoples from the Mediterranean world met the Cimbri with whom they were later to get much better acquainted.

While on his expedition, Pytheas, like any good scientist, kept conscientious notes which he ultimately wrote up into a text called 'About the Ocean'. Most of this text has been lost, but occasional snippets have been preserved as extracts in the surviving writings of geographers of the ancient world. Thus, we know that at some point Pytheas took his ship along the northwest coast of Europe and came to a point which he called Mentonomon, at the tip of a peninsula which today we call Jutland, in modern Denmark.

In antiquity this land was later called the 'Cimbric Chersonese', and there Pytheas discovered that amber was so common that 'the natives use this as fuel and sell it to their neighbours, the Teutones.' (Pytheas as quoted in Pliny, *Natural Histories* 325.) This text is significant as it gives the earliest reported geographical location of the Teutones, a people who, like the Cimbri, were later to become a major threat to Rome. That the 'natives' described by Pytheas were indeed the Cimbri becomes more probable after an examination of another writer of the fourth century BC called Ephorus. Ephorus describes the attributes of two groups whom he describes as living in close proximity – the Cimbri and Teutones. Thus, from the combined evidence of these ancient writers, we can be reasonably sure that the Cimbri and Teutones were established on the north of the Jutland peninsula for at least two centuries before they began their historic march on Rome.

Based upon this information, ancient and modern historians have combined to produce an interesting hypothesis. Half a millennium before the Cimbri appear in the historical record, the Assyrian empire was troubled by a wave of barbarian Celtic warriors called the Cimmerians (a people best known today through a fictional sword-and-sorcery hero from that tribe called Conan the Barbarian). No-one knows where these Cimmerian invaders came from, but Homer (*Odyssey* 11.13) informs us that they came from a mist-filled land beside the Ocean 'where the sun never rises, even at midday'.

Thus there exists a tantalizing possibility that the Cimbri were the legendary Cimmerians, and some etymologists have experimented with torturing proto-Celtic to see whether the word 'Cimmerian' might have mutated over the centuries into the word 'Cimbri'. There are however many more credible origins for that word, and it has often been noted that another Celtic people call themselves something very similar – the Cymru, also known as the Welsh. Rather than stretching for an origin among the Cimmerians, one might turn to the more securely established word-root 'cimb', which refers to a prisoner taken for ransom. Or, more probably in the case of the Cimbri, 'those who take prisoners for ransom', because the German peoples who lived south of the Cimbri seem to have suffered from the predatory behaviour of their northern neighbours long before the Romans did.

The ancient etymologist Festus remarks bluntly that 'In the language of the Gauls [i.e. Celtic] the word for 'brigands' is Cimbri'. To this we can add the speculations of Plutarch, the biographer who wrote of the Cimbri in his *Life of Marius* that

> it could not be ascertained what people they were nor from where they had originated … The most common theory was that they were of the Germanic peoples who reach as far as the northern ocean, a supposition based on their great stature, their light-blue eyes, and the fact that 'Cimbri' is what the Germans call bandits. (Plutarch, *Marius*, 11.3)

So from here we can claim with considerable certainty that the Cimbri were a folk who lived with their neighbours the Teutones in northern Jutland and had done so since at least the third century BC. The next question, and one which considerably troubled ethnologists of the nineteenth century, is whether we should consider the Cimbri as Celts or Germans? Given that even other barbarians considered the Cimbri somewhat barbaric it might be considered somewhat odd that the Germans of the nineteenth century made a strong pitch for the Cimbri to be considered as one of their own – a position probably based upon the then-popular idea that the German *volk* represented an alternative culture to the Mediterranean values espoused by the Greeks and Romans.

There are certainly good grounds for arguing that the Cimbri were a Germanic tribe – everyone else in the region was a German, so if the Cimbri were Celtic this would make them an island of foreigners in a Germanic sea. Also, the Cimbri are described as large, lanky, and with such flaxen hair that the hair of their children appeared to be white. This is in contrast to the average Celt, who had dark or reddish hair depending on the sub-genotype, but the Cimbric hair colouration is common enough among Germans ancient and modern. As we have seen, Plutarch reckoned the Cimbri were Germans, as does the historian Appian, and so also does Julius Caesar, who was born only a few years after the Cimbric menace had been thrown back from Rome and who may well have encountered the children of Cimbric prisoners.

Yet as an early modern historian has sourly remarked, Caesar the writer is as unparalleled as Caesar the general, but Caesar the ethnographer is a less convincing character (Canon Rawlinson 'On the Ethnography of the Cimbri', *Journal of the Anthropological Institute of Great Britain and Ireland*, Vol. 6 1877, pp. 150–158). Also (he goes on to say) no-one has any difficulty with the concrete reality of the Galatians. These were a Celtic people who ended up ensconced in the Anatolian highlands (of modern Turkey) as an island of Celts in a sea of even more foreign foreigners. It may seem improbable that a Celtic people could find so distant and alien a homeland, yet no-one believes that St Paul wrote his famous letter to a figment of his imagination.

So there is nothing intrinsically incredible in the theory that invading Celts might have muscled their way into the Jutland peninsula, especially if they allied – as they did – with the neighbouring Teutones, about whose ethnicity there is nowhere near enough evidence to even speculate.

A lot of work has been done on the genetic make-up of the Cimbri in an attempt to determine their exact ethnicity, and whether any of their alleged descendants share the same genes. In this scientific quest, Exhibit A is an individual known as 'Tolland Man'. Mr Tolland is aged somewhere between 35 and 45 years old. He is somewhat unshaven, has short-cropped hair worn under a conical sheepskin cap, sunken eyes and an aquiline nose. He is also something like 2,300 years old, meaning that he might have been around when Pytheas came to visit his homeland while on his northern exploratory expedition.

We know of Tolland man because he was hanged and his body was cast into the Bjaeldskoval peat bog. Peat bogs are acidic and anaerobic, meaning that they do not support the usual bacteria which consume human corpses within a few years, and so Tolland man was found in a state of near-complete preservation. (Which did not survive his exhumation – the body rotted away, but the head was removed and preserved.)

Because the Bjaeldskoval peat bog lies well within what should have been the lands of the Cimbri, this well-preserved corpse has enough DNA to give scientists a near-complete genome. In fact, enough of the corpse was preserved to allow for analysis of the hair and stomach contents to tell what the man last ate and where he had been in the last year. (This latter because hair preserves strontium levels, and these are different in different parts of Denmark.) Yet for all this abundance of information, Tolland man's DNA has made little contribution to debate as to the ethnicity of the Cimbri. This is because Tolland man's DNA does not contain markers which would make him a good match with any of his presumed later relatives either in Denmark or other parts of Europe where the Cimbri are believed to have ended up. On the other hand, his DNA is not distinctively Germanic either.

This unhelpful DNA may be explained by the fact that the man, who appears to have been aristocratic, may have been the product of tribal intermarriage, (strontium levels in his hair show that he had travelled widely in Denmark), or he may not even have been Cimbric, but a ritually-sacrificed prisoner. It is known, for example that the Cimbri were fond of disembowelling prisoners and draining their blood in order to divine the will of their gods, so this supposed 'first of the Cimbri' might have actually been a foreign hostage who paid the price of a diplomatic deal gone wrong.

If DNA studies have not yet provided a definitive answer, archaeology at least provides abundant evidence that the Cimbri were Celtic. For example, the Danish peat bogs have been revealing in other ways apart from the bodies that they have preserved for posterity. The Cimbri deposited more than corpses into their murky depths; cauldrons, weapons and jewellery have also been found. The similarity of these artefacts with others that archaeologists have unearthed in indisputably Celtic territory make it certain that the Cimbri were Celtic by culture no matter what their genetic make-up might have been. The famous Gundrstrup Cauldron, for example, shows typical Celtic warriors with oblong shields and the dragon's head trumpets of a type described by the Romans who later met them in combat. Likewise, two wagons found in another peat bog (the Dejbjerg wagons) seem to be of typical Celtic design.

Returning to the historical record, it seems that less than a generation after the Greek explorer Pytheas visited the Cimbri in their northern fastness, the Cimbri returned the compliment by visiting the Greeks. In 279 BC a huge barbarian army descended upon Greece, intent upon plunder. Though usually on a smaller scale, such raids were not uncommon, as the unfortunate Macedonians could testify. A surprising amount of co-ordination took place among tribal leaders beforehand and as a result very diverse tribes might join forces to attack their southern neighbours.

There are strong indications that the Cimbri joined one such confederation which made up an army almost 100,000 strong and also included Gauls and Illyrians. In his text on the Illyrian wars, the historian Appian mentions an Illyrian tribe called the Autarienses who 'were destroyed by the vengeance of Apollo for having joined Molostimus and the Celtic people called the Cimbri in an expedition against the temple of Delphi.' (Appian, *Illyrian Wars* 1.4)

As it happens, this raid was a failure and the invasion force was thrown back from Delphi and handed a devastating defeat by the Greeks at Thermopylae. Nevertheless, of interest in that statement by Appian are two details, the first being that their participation in this huge incursion confirms that the Cimbri were indeed the predatory raiders that the Germans considered them to be.

The second detail is that Appian later reports that, like the ill-fated Autarienses mentioned above, the Cimbri also were subject to the vengeance of Apollo. This latter point is significant because Apollo seems to have liked revenge as a dish served very cold. Apparently, he stayed his wrath for two generations before unleashing his fury upon the third, and in doing so precipitated the mass tribal movement which set the Cimbri on a collision course with Rome.

The form taken by the alleged vengeance of Apollo was less typical of the methods of that god (who liked to smite his enemies with a vicious plague or two), than with the *modus operandi* of earth-shaking Poseidon, who liked to bury his victims under a tsunami. There is good reason to believe that just such a natural disaster (whether or not divinely inspired) hit and temporarily submerged much of the Cimbric homeland at around the time just before their migration.

That Jutland could have been swamped by a tsunami is documented by the geographer Strabo, even as he denies that such a thing was possible.

> Clitarchus [a historian whose works are now lost] must be wrong when he says that [Cimbric] horsemen rode away when they saw the waters rising, and though they were in full gallop they came close to being caught by the flood. In the first place we know that the tide never comes in that fast ... and secondly that the tide comes in on a daily basis and people accustomed to hearing and seeing the sea's imperceptible encroachment would not regard this as something unexpected that would cause them to flee in terror. (Strabo, *Geography* 7.2.1)

As Strabo points out, the usual changing of the tides would have occasioned no alarm at all among the Cimbri, so what is being described above is something completely different, and what fits that description best is a tsunami. (Another possibility is a large-scale storm flood, to which the Jutland region has always been prone. The later written record contains numerous instances where a combination of a high tide and high winds in just the wrong direction have caused large-scale flooding.)

A disastrous tsunami need not have been accompanied by an earthquake, for the area is not one of great seismic activity. Sea levels in the region are known to have fluctuated greatly, and such a fluctuation may have triggered an undersea landslide, which would be more than sufficient to cause a massive wave from which even horsemen might struggle to escape.

Also of interest is an undersea feature known as the 'Storegga slides', a series of undersea landslips off the coast of Norway which have definitely caused massive tsunamis in the past. It may well be that a similar disaster wiped out the Cimbric homeland. (Significantly, the last of the Storegga slides is reckoned to have happened around 2,200 years ago – just as our putative tsunami hit the Jutland coast and devastated the lands of the Cimbri.)

The catastrophic flood theory is also supported by those faithful historians, Denmark's peat bogs. At one point in the Iron Age some of these bogs developed a layer of sand and gravel, exactly the sort of thing that would be swept over the bog if carried by a massive surge of seawater. It certainly did not help the Cimbri that their part of Jutland was flat and swampy to begin with. Indeed, part of Jutland became an island after 1825 when storm floods permanently separated part of the landmass from the mainland.

The problem with such a flood – disastrous as it would have been – lay not so much in the immediate destruction of homes and a single harvest, but in the fact that this part of Jutland was so poorly drained. The waves would not have washed back as the causes of the disaster receded but instead the salt-laden waters would have settled into the ground, thus ruining it for agriculture in an area where most farming was marginal at the best of times. In short, this calamity made it imperative for almost the entire nation of the Cimbri to abandon their homes and move away in search of a new homeland. With their fields ruined, they could not stay where they were, so their choices were move or starve.

In their forced migration the Cimbri were accompanied by many from the neighbouring nation of the Teutones, either because the Teutones saw a chance to profit from the chaos which would undoubtedly follow the march of the Cimbri, or because they also were in a similar plight. (The Greek gods were not known to be discriminating in their wrath.)

When exactly this migration began is uncertain, though somewhere around 120 BC seems a reasonable date. Again, the number of Cimbri on the move is also uncertain, though most historians agree that Plutarch's estimate of 300,000 warriors – let alone the non-combatants – is most probably an over-estimate. (The Romans rather liked to overstate the size of opposing armies, all the better to emphasize their own martial valour.)

That said, there were certainly enough Cimbri and Teutones to cause huge disruption in the lands through which they passed. It is in fact likely that one reason Julius Caesar was originally able to get a foothold in Gaul was because the ripples of peoples displaced or disturbed by the passage of the Cimbri two generations before were still making themselves felt.

That the movement of one tribe could displace several others is due to what has been colourfully described as the 'billiard-ball' theory of tribal movement. That is, a tribe displaced as the marauding Cimbri moved through their territory might descend en masse upon the lands of a neighbour, and remain there after finding these lands more congenial than their own. The dispossessed in turn sought refuge elsewhere or to tried displace weaker neighbours. The entire ripple effect played out over decades through tribal raids, battles and massacres.

Certainly, the Gaul described by Caesar was an unsettled place where the Romans were able to use the large-scale movement of various peoples to their own advantage by exploiting the tribal divisions and the present and historical resentments that these movements had caused. (One benefit of the Cimbric migration for posterity was a large increase in buried treasure along their route. Very often the owners never returned for it, much to the delight of treasure-hunters and archaeologists.)

From what we can establish, the first steps of the migrating horde from Jutland took them down the Amber Road – a route which operated in much the same way as the more famous Silk Road. While the Silk Road brought precious goods from China and the Orient westwards to the Mediterranean, the Amber Road ran mostly north to south. For hundreds of years goods which were passed from one trader to the other as Baltic amber were funnelled to places such as Assyria and Egypt. (For example, Baltic amber was found among the grave goods of the deceased pharaoh Tutankhamen, who died in the fourteenth century BC.)

Thus, the first tribes to feel the pain of the Cimbric odyssey were those living along the Amber Road in what today we would call northern Germany and western Poland. This route took the migrants through the Koldzko Valley and down towards the Danube. This would have been familiar territory for those raised on tales of the Cimbric attack on Delphi, for the original Cimbric raiding horde must have followed much the same path.

The problem with this path is that it eventually took the Cimbri into the territory of the Illyrian tribes of what is today Croatia. When they were not looking for allies to help them assault their Greek neighbours, the people of this region weren't very fond of uninvited guests and had no inhibitions about showing it. Generally speaking, the land of Illyria is remarkably mountainous and so unsupportive of agriculture that the inland inhabitants were mainly pastoral, and those on the coast were notorious for supplementing their incomes through piracy.

Faced with the prospect of unrelenting hostility from people very good at warfare and the dubious reward of settling in territory barely worth having, the Cimbri reasonably decided to turn again to the northwest. There is also a suggestion that at this time the Illyrians were suffering from a plague of some description, and the Cimbri either caught it, or headed away fast to avoid catching it.

This move brought the Cimbri into contact with their distant Celtic cousins, the Boii. The Boii were dispersed across a wide region between Noricum and Illyria and their name survives today in the territory of Bohemia (Boii + heim = home of the Boii). The Boii were already well-known to the Romans whom they regularly terrorized with large-scale raids into northeast Italy. The Boii had recently expanded towards the Veneto, and had joyfully joined forces with Hannibal in 218 BC to further trouble their Roman neighbours. The Romans attempted to do something about this in 216 BC by dispatching an army under the consul Postuimus Albinus to take care of the problem. How successful Albinus was in this venture is best demonstrated by the fact that the now-deceased consul's gold-plated skull was subsequently used as a drinking bowl by the victorious Boii.

As can be imagined, any warrior people who were capable of fighting off the Roman military machine were no pushover, even for a race of warriors as dedicated and ferocious as the Cimbri. (The Romans finally vanquished the Boii in the early Imperial period.) We know almost nothing of the Cimbric-Boii war, though it must have been an epic affair that seems to have ended in a winning draw for the Boii. We can tentatively assume this because the Cimbri did not settle in the rather desirable lands which the Boii occupied along the Danube in what later became Pannonia, but instead continued with their migration. On the other hand, by the time they came into bruising contact with the

Romans, the Cimbric leader called himself Boiorix, or 'King of the Boii'. This suggests that the Boii might have offered a nominal submission in order to encourage the Cimbri to move elsewhere with their pride intact.

From their route it seems that the Cimbri were looking to settle among their fellow Celts, and from the archaeological evidence of abandoned hill-fort towns along their route, it seems that potential hosts either cleared out on the approach of the Cimbri or did the opposite and opportunistically joined the migration to see where it might lead. Where that migration led, around six years after their migration had begun, was to the lands of a mountain people called the Scordisci.

The Scordisci could not resist the invading horde, not least because they were already fighting a long-running war with the Romans on their western front. The Cimbric leadership realized that if they bulldozed right through the Scordisci they would run right into the armies of Rome. The Cimbri were no fools and they certainly knew that the Romans were a militaristic people who had already conquered Macedon, subdued Greece, obliterated Carthage, and handed the mighty Seleucid empire a string of military defeats. Unwilling to risk a confrontation with so great a power, the Cimbri swerved instead into the lands of the Taurisci, a people who dwelt in what today is northern Slovenia.

The Taurisci were as happy to see the Cimbri as had been everyone else whom the migrants had encountered on their travels, which is to say not happy at all. Fortunately, though not themselves a particularly powerful tribe, the Taurisci had formidable allies – those very Romans whom the Cimbri were seeking to avoid. For the Romans it hardly seemed in doubt that their nation (which had, after all, humbled the greatest powers in the Mediterranean world) would have no difficulty quashing a horde of half-naked savages from the far north. Accordingly, when they received panicked requests for aid from ambassadors from the Taurisci, the Roman army turned northeast to put the matter to the test.

Chapter 2

Rome – a City for Sale

From the exploits of the Cimbri we now turn to the Romans who opposed them. At this time the Roman Republic was both a rising power and a declining one, for success abroad was balanced by increasing dysfunction at home. While the armies of the Republic had carried the standards of Rome to the Atlantic coast and to the mountains of Armenia, the social cohesion upon which Roman military might was based had been coming unglued for decades, and this dysfunction had reached the point where it had seriously begun to interfere with Rome's ability to make war.

Therefore, before we come to the first confrontation with the Cimbri, we need to briefly examine what had happened to the state which had conquered Hannibal and see where it stood both in terms of its overseas engagements and in terms of domestic democratic collapse. It will quickly become evident that the state which was busily ruining the lives of others through continual campaigns of expansion and conquest was far from a happy place itself.

The fundamental problem underlying Rome's social difficulties was that the sixteen-year-long war with Hannibal between 218 and 201 BC had inflicted lasting wounds upon the Roman Republic. Arguably these were wounds which never healed, and which were certainly still negatively affecting the Republic a century later. The costs of the Hannibalic war were huge, both in money and manpower, and while Rome's financial ills were redressed relatively easily with booty from the conquered, not much could be done about the fact that an estimated one in every four adult Roman males had perished in the war, with lower but still massive casualties affecting the rest of Italy.

The human cost of the war was especially high in southern Italy where Hannibal's and Rome's armies had sparred ineffectively for over a decade and a half. During this time both sides helped themselves to the crops and livestock of the peasantry and any adult male capable of working the fields was also deemed capable of being forcibly conscripted into fighting for one side or the other. As a result, one problem facing the Romans after their war with Hannibal was a large-scale agricultural manpower shortage, a shortage which was particularly felt in the devastated south.

Yet, despite this, barely had the war with Carthage come to an end than the Senate decided to go to war with king Philip V of Macedon. It is reasonable to assume that one reason for this was that Macedon was a wealthy state and Rome needed money. Another reason was that when the Romans had reached their darkest hour in the war against Hannibal, Philip V and the Macedonians had (in the Romans' opinion) stabbed them in the back. This was in 216 BC, just after Hannibal's epic victory at Cannae, when the Romans had lost close to 70,000 men in a single afternoon. As Rome was recovering from news of the disaster, the city received the further news that Philip of Macedon had declared war.

No matter that Philip probably regarded Hannibal's war with Rome as over apart from the negotiations for Rome's inevitable surrender, and that Philip was primarily interested in Hannibal's co-operation in his continual feud with his Hellenistic rivals. No matter also that Philip did very little to help Carthage as the war turned against Hannibal – and no matter either that by 201 BC Macedon and Rome had already patched up a peace (the Peace of Phoenice) which allowed the Romans to concentrate single-mindedly on Carthage. The fact was that Philip was now top of the Senate's 'to do' list, and barely was the ink dry on Carthage's surrender than the Senate declared war on Philip.

Or rather the Senate tried to do this. The problem for the Senate was that Rome was – however nominally – a democracy. It was the Roman people who decided whether or not Rome went to war, and the Roman people didn't want to. The gathering of voters who decided upon such issues was called the *comitia comitata*, and when they were called upon, the Roman people voted decisively against war. Using a tactic that has been repeatedly used in democracies in the centuries thereafter, the governing class refused to take no for an answer, and made it plain that the Roman people would be repeatedly polled until they came up with the 'right' response. Eventually the Romans voted – reluctantly – for war.

The significance of this vote was that it was a further demonstration of the fact that in the Roman Republic the Senate – technically an advisory body with very limited constitutional power – was actually the tail that wagged the Roman dog. This would be less of an issue were it not for the fact that members of the Senate were increasingly preoccupied with their own power and status and ever less concerned with the welfare of the Republic as a whole.

Thus we see neither surprise nor great indignation at the political antics of Flamininus, the general in charge of the latter part of the war against Philip V of Macedon. Philip had never wanted a renewed war with Rome and, after a number of setbacks against the Romans, he was keen to make peace. At the same time, Flamininus was facing a vote as to whether his command of the war against Philip was to be extended.

Flamininus wrote to his friends and instructed them that if his command was not extended they should join the peace faction in the Senate, so that when Flamininus entered into talks with Philip, he might have the prestige of ending the war. If his command was extended then the supporters of Flamininus should back the war party, so that Flamininus could garner the glory of a military victory over the Macedonians.

Thus the issue of peace or war, and the lives and deaths of thousands of men, was decided not on the basis of what was good for the Roman Republic, but purely on the basis of what was good for the political career of Titus Flamininus. This was just one example of a pattern of behaviour that the Roman aristocracy were to repeat with distressing frequency in the decades that followed.

Another issue to note was that while campaigning in Greece, the Romans demonstrated a degree of perfidy which was to become something of a trademark for a state which had once prided itself on moral rectitude. The people of Epirus had supported Macedon, which left them in a vulnerable position after Philip was eventually defeated. (Flamininus got the extension of his command that he wanted.)

As part of the peace with Macedon, Rome had agreed to withdraw all its troops from Greece. There were a substantial number of troops posted near Epirus, and the commander there told the Epirots that the Romans had decided – in return for a vast ransom of bullion – to leave the Epirot cities free and ungarrisoned. Thereafter, in a perfectly synchronized manoeuvre, Roman troops turned up in seventy locations in Epirus on the same day. The legionaries first collected the ransom then turned upon the Epirot citizens, sacked the towns and enslaved the inhabitants. In that one operation some 150,000 men, women and children were captured and brought back to Italy.

Many of these slaves were used to restock the ranks of the devastated farm workers who had perished in the Hannibalic war. However, these workers were not free peasants as formerly, but slaves who worked upon huge consolidated estates called *latifundia* and treated basically as human livestock. The land had been mostly purchased as war-devastated property at fire-sale prices by the Roman aristocracy after the Hannibalic war, or simply taken over as vacant possessions, the previous owners having vanished without trace. One aspect which infuriated the soldiery of Rome and the city's allies was that sometimes wealthy Romans took over smallholdings by force.

The landowners could not complain because at the time they were away in the army fighting for Rome, and when they returned to find themselves dispossessed they had to challenge the usurpation of their land. The problem was that disputes over land titles had to be settled in the courts, and those courts were controlled by the friends or clients of those who had done the usurping, so dispossessed landowners seldom got the justice they were seeking. Through the same mixture of bribery, usurpation and judicial collusion many Roman aristocrats simply took over public land ostensibly owned by the Roman state and treated it as their own, farming the land, building on it and passing it down through inheritance.

As a result of enrichment through these quasi-legal and downright illegal shenanigans, and also because of the plunder from the Macedonian wars, serious amounts of money now entered Roman politics. This mattered because obtaining high office in Rome was already an expensive business, albeit one which offered substantial rewards on the high initial investment. To become a serious contender for high office a senator had to first be elected to a series of lesser offices, each with an associated set of electoral expenses.

This ascending list of magistracies was called the *cursus honorum*, and it was less a ladder than a pyramid. The most junior magistracy was quaestor, and the most senior was consul. Ten quaestors were elected each year, but only two consuls, (while two censors – arguably as powerful – were chosen only once every five years). In other words, there was considerable attrition along the road to the top offices, and politicians fought like rabid dogs not to be among the casualties.

A candidate for high office needed to cultivate influential friends with gifts and loans, and to entertain top people with expensive dinners, events and parties. He also needed to impress the voters with his generosity, his dedication to public works and his willingness to throw expensive entertainments in the amphitheatre and circus.

Once their ethically dubious property investments started to yield substantial benefits, some Roman aristocrats started to gain a serious financial advantage over their peers. Being able to afford more lavish election campaigns, these aristocrats gained an increasingly tight grip on the top offices of state and the huge rewards thereof. This spiral of ever-increasing wealth among a diminishing few meant that the top offices in Rome became largely restricted to just a few families. These were the men whom Cicero was later to describe as 'made consuls in their cradles', so certain were they of getting the top jobs when they grew up. However, competition remained intense, and the cost of election campaigns kept increasing.

Therefore, even if of a wealthy family, once in office a consul was often also deeply in debt. Fortunately, a consul was also a war leader, and his need for money could be met by the booty extracted from successful campaigns against Rome's enemies. (Although some of these involuntary donations came from people who did not even know they were Rome's enemies until a money-hungry consul attacked them.) A consul could also extort considerable sums from the people of the province which he governed.

A generation later, the orator Cicero put together a comprehensive list of gubernatorial malfeasances perpetrated by Verres, governor of Sicily, but most of these abuses of authority were already being practised before the Cimbric wars began in 110 BC. As the saying went, a man seriously interested in politics needed to accumulate three fortunes – one to get himself elected to office in the first place, one to bribe jurors when outraged provincials afterwards charged him with extortion, and one for himself to gain leverage from loans and bribes to promising candidates for office in the next generation.

Some reformers made determined efforts to stop the rot. The most notable attempt was made in the generation before the Cimbric wars, and despite huge popular support very little was achieved against the monolithic opposition of a Senate dedicated to preserving the short-term interests of its members.

The reformers were themselves aristocrats – two brothers, Tiberius and Gaius Gracchus – who aimed to take away the power of the wealthiest senators by redistributing the land which they had seized illegally. Also as a check on the Senate, the Gracchi promoted the powers of the class just below the senators, the equestrians. The success of the reformers can be judged by the fact that both Tiberius and Gaius died violently – with Tiberius actually being lynched by a mob of senators and their assistants who attacked him while he was addressing the Roman people. Meanwhile, the equestrians proved to be as cynical and money-hungry as the Senate, and their malign influence in the courts (where equestrians now composed some of the juries) helped to bring the reputation of Roman justice to a new low.

By this time Rome's senators were a cynical and self-interested oligarchy, and since oligarchies tend by definition to be exclusive, men of talent were often locked out of the top jobs. Since the very top job was consul and the consul was also a war leader, this meant that Rome's armies were often led by men who were second-rate at best and utterly incompetent at worst. Generals desperate for money and glory but lacking the ability properly to lead their armies was not a good combination. Add to that shameless cynicism and a (justified) belief that members of the oligarchy could literally get away with murder and it becomes evident why Rome's reputation and military prowess went into steep decline between the Hannibalic and Cimbric wars. Some examples might illustrate this.

The highly aristocratic Servius Sulpicius Galba was praetor (the rank just below consul) in 151 BC. He led the Roman effort in Spain against the Lusitanian people, demonstrating his military incompetence in his first battle where he was comprehensively defeated with the loss of thousands of men. Rather than fight another battle, in the next year Galba entered into negotiations with the Lusitanians. Claiming that he now understood that a shortage of land lay behind the Lusitanians warlike raiding, Galba offered them land in exchange for peace. The Lusitanians jumped at the offer once they heard that would-be settlers would get grants of new territory within Spain. On an agreed day, thousands of Lusitanians – in fact most of the tribe – turned up to be relocated. The Romans divided the crowd into three groups and disarmed anyone carrying a weapon. With the Lusitanians split up and defenceless, Galba ordered his men to fall upon the helpless mass of people and massacre them all.

When put on trial for this egregious violation of Roman *fides* (good faith), Galba did not even try to defend himself. Instead he presented his children to the court and tearfully asked the jury what his innocent babes would do if he were exiled. The jury, swayed by compassion and by the huge amounts of money that Galba had bestowed upon them in bribes, voted to let him go unpunished. Meanwhile, back in Iberia Rome paid the price for Galba's betrayal with a savage guerrilla war fought by outraged Lusitanian survivors, which dragged on for generations. (One of Galba's descendants briefly became emperor in AD 68.)

We can pass over other examples of broken promises, treaty violations, bad faith and massacre in Spain, as these pale into insignificance when compared with the even-more-blatant examples of greed and corruption demonstrated by the Roman oligarchy during the Jugurthine War, which began brewing just as the Cimbri were leaving their homeland in Jutland.

This war and the lead-up to its declaration are eloquently described by the historian Sallust – a man who turned to writing history because he found that he lacked the money and connections to get far in politics. Sallust was understandably bitter about this and he wrote *Jugurthine War* partly as a savage indictment of the Roman ruling class.

We learn that Jugurtha was the adopted son of Micipsa, king of Numidia in North Africa. Micipsa's father Masinissa had been a steadfast ally of Rome in the Hannibalic war, and young Jugurtha himself had served in Spain with Scipio Aemilianus, who was perhaps the only competent Roman commander to campaign there in the previous two decades. It is said that after publicly commending Jugurtha for his outstanding performance in the war, Scipio took the young man aside and privately warned him about the limits of ambition.

If this warning was indeed delivered, Jugurtha treated it as he did all subsequent warnings from the Romans – that is to say, he ignored it completely. When King Micipsa died, he left his country to be divided among his heirs, one of whom was Jugurtha. Jugurtha expressed his dissatisfaction with this arrangement by killing one of his two co-monarchs soon after his coronation. With one rival down and one to go, Jugurtha declared war upon Adherbal, his surviving rival, and defeated him in battle. The hapless Adherbal fled to Rome and appealed for a settlement.

Roman officials duly arrived and opened negotiations – that is to say, they settled down to discuss how much it would take to bribe them and what the bribes would purchase. Among these corrupt officials was one Opimius, a senator who had been instrumental in engineering the downfall and killing of the reforming Gaius Gracchus. After due deliberation, the suddenly-much-richer Roman delegation decided that Jugurtha should be punished for his murderous aggression by being awarded half of Numidia (there is some dispute among modern academics as to whether this was the richer half as the Roman sources claim), while Adherbal took the other half.

This settlement was accompanied by a stern warning that Jugurtha should henceforth make an effort to keep the peace. Sadly for the delegation, the Roman people later looked at what the envoys to Numidia had actually done rather than their airy declarations about making a lasting peace, and a subsequent commission of enquiry discovered enough damning evidence of corruption to send Opimius into exile. (It should be noted that this condemnation was not due to a sudden outbreak of morality in Rome. Opimius was exiled because Gaius Gracchus was a Roman aristocrat, and he had family and friends who were still outraged by his death. The Romans took their political feuds very seriously, and Opimius' blatant acceptance of bribes gave his enemies the opportunity to destroy him.)

Nevertheless, in Africa the damage had been done and no-one talked of depriving Jugurtha of his ill-gotten gains. Indeed, had Jugurtha thereafter kept to the terms of the peace deal, then the settlement would probably have been a short footnote in most history books. Instead Jugurtha decided that he was not going to settle for half a kingdom when he could take it all. The renegade king took Rome's de facto acquiescence in his killing of one co-monarch as evidence that he could probably get away with another attempt at killing the other – that is, provided he had the funds on hand to pay off whomever was in power in Rome at the time that he did it.

Accordingly, in 112 BC Jugurtha dispatched bribes to Rome and an army to Adherbal's territory. The judicious application of those bribes to cash-starved aristocrats created a 'peace faction' within the Roman Senate. Thereafter, judicious filibusters and procedural delays in the Senate blocked Roman attempts at intervention in Africa while Jugurtha ripped up Adherbal's army and pinned him in his capital, the city of Cirta. There Jugurtha's defeated co-monarch held out at the urging of the large population of Roman and Italian businessmen in the city. These men were naively sure that Jugurtha's flagrant violation of the previous peace deal meant that help would be forthcoming from Rome, any day now.

Instead, the Senate sent a delegation urging Jugurtha to mend his ways. Jugurtha listened politely and informed the envoys that 'he took the the will of the Roman Senate very seriously, and that nothing was more important to him than that' (Sallust, *Jugurthine War* 22). Then he proceeded to disregard everything the delegates had told him and got on with the siege of Cirta.

Though trapped in Cirta, Adherbal managed to get a desperate message to Rome, pointing out that Jugurtha had blatantly broken his promises to the Roman delegation and that Cirta was about to fall. Sallust documented the Roman senate's response.

> There was a group that wanted Jugurtha's disregard of the envoys to be noted, and that an army should be sent to Africa to aid Adherbal. But those people organized by Jugurtha did everything in their power to prevent the passing of such a decree, and in the end private interests [in the Senate] prevailed over the public good – as was often the case. Instead another delegation was sent to Africa, this time composed of men of the highest rank and standing. (Sallust, *Jugurthine War* 25)

Jugurtha again took time off from the siege of Cirta to attend to the Roman delegation, listen politely to their 'terrible threats' and then ignore them completely. That is not to say that the delegations' presence achieved nothing. The Italians and Romans in Cirta, certain that even Jugurtha would not dare to act too unreasonably with senior Roman diplomats nearby to bear witness to his misdeeds, arranged a peace deal whereby the city would surrender to Jugurtha, but Adherbal would be allowed to go free to present his case to the Senate.

Adherbal agreed with extreme reluctance and then only because he was dependent on the Italians and Romans for the defence of the city. His reservations were promptly proven correct. Once the town had surrendered, Jugurtha promptly killed most of the male inhabitants – including any Romans and Italians he thought were part of Cirta's defence. Adherbal was not allowed to go free as Jugurtha had promised but was instead slowly and carefully tortured to death.

Even then, says Sallust, 'so great was the power of the king's influence and money that his partisans in the Senate might have drawn out discussion and debate until public indignation had dissipated and nothing need be done.' However, a tribune of the plebs indignant at the massacre of Romans and Italians at Cirta raised a public outcry demanding that something should be done. Eventually, and reluctantly, the Senate dispatched an army to deal with the man whom so many still favoured.

The Roman army arrived in Numidia and commenced hostilities with considerable success against Jugurtha's men – but against Jugurtha's money the Roman commanders were helpless. Within a very short time Jugurtha had enthusiastically surrendered to Rome. He handed over thirty elephants and a small sum of silver to the Roman state and in return was confirmed in his position as king of Numidia. In other words, his defiance of the Senate, his disregard of previous peace deals, his massacre of Romans and Italians and his takeover of the kingdom by killing the other two legitimate heirs – all of these offences were covered by the payment of a trivial indemnity to the Roman state.

The news that Jugurtha had gotten away with his crimes after receiving the lightest of slaps on the wrist was greeted with popular indignation in Rome. It was suspected – with very probable justification – that the money that Jugurtha had paid to the Roman treasury was a mere pittance compared to the sums he had expended in bribing Rome's commanders and the diplomats with whom he had arranged the terms of his 'surrender'.

> Don't let this wickedness go unpunished. This is not just a case of embezzling public money, or of extorting gold from our allies. Those might be serious crimes, but they are so common that these days we pay them little attention. Instead consider how the Senate has prostituted itself to a bloodthirsty enemy. The will of the Roman people has been betrayed and clearly Rome is now for sale both at home and abroad. (Sallust, *Jugurthine War* 31)

Thus Sallust reports the outraged speech of an angry tribune. Yet, while Rome's commanders probably took the bribes that Jugurtha offered, modern historians doubt that these men were influenced by the lure of gold alone. They may have had grave doubts about the advisability of fighting a war against a relatively unimportant African nation to the south, and doing so at a time when a threat had manifested in the north that threatened the very survival of the Roman state.

The Cimbri had arrived.

Chapter 3

Rome Versus the Cimbri –
Sizing Up the Opposition

In the year 114 BC, the year when the Cimbri first appeared north of the Roman frontier, the city was gripped by a terrible presentiment of doom. The Romans liked to think of their community – all 394,336 citizens according to their latest census – as a large family. Watching over this family was Vesta, goddess of home and hearth. Should Vesta become upset with the Romans and withdraw her protection, the Romans were sure that their city was doomed. Of all the things that were likely to offend Vesta, one of the worst was if the Vestal Virgins who guarded the sacred fire in her shrine were to allow the flames to die out. The very worst thing was if it turned out that the Vestal Virgins weren't.

In fact, according to some sources – albeit vitriolically anti-Senate sources – Vestal Virgins had been misbehaving for years, and their misconduct was tolerated by the senatorial aristocracy from whose families the Vestals were generally drawn. (In the mind of the average Roman this might explain the mediocre performance of Roman armies over the previous decade.) This benign neglect of laws enforcing the chastity of the Vestals was overturned by a slave called Manius.

Manius had for some time been the go-between who arranged liaisons between the highly aristocratic Vestal 'Virgin' Aemilia and her clandestine lover. As a reward for helping to perpetrate this sacrilege, Manius was promised his freedom, a promise made as often as delivery of that promise was postponed. Eventually, well aware that he faced torture and execution should Aemilia's affair come to light, Manius tired of his high-risk lifestyle, took himself to the authorities and comprehensively denounced his mistress' conduct.

The denunciation was made so publicly that there was no way to hush it up. The subsequent investigation revealed not only that Aemilia had been repeatedly unchaste, but that two of her colleagues, Licinia and Marcia, had also taken lovers. The panel of investigators decided that Aemilia was the most guilty of the Vestals, for not only had she been the first to break her vows, but she had encouraged her colleagues to do the same. The problem was how Aemilia should be punished.

Despite her abject failure to keep to her sacred oaths, Aemilia was still a Vestal, and that meant that her person was sacrosanct. Apart from getting a whipping should she allow the sacred fire to go out, the law forbade that any Vestal be harmed either within Rome or outside the city's walls. This was the sort of challenge that the legalistic Roman mind could not resist. In the end Aemilia was executed by being given plenty of food and drink, but she was entombed with those rations within a sealed chamber inside the city walls themselves. There she presumably later died in darkness and silence. As tradition dictated, her lover was burned alive in the Roman forum. The other two Vestals were adjudged to have committed lesser crimes and were pardoned.

The Roman people saw the pardoning of these Vestals as yet another example of a corrupt Roman aristocracy protecting its own. So great was the public outcry that eventually Licinia and Marcia were also entombed and another bonfire lit in the forum. That ended the matter on the mortal plane, but the question now preoccupying Roman minds was whether they had done enough to appease the anger of the gods. Had Vesta been satisfied by the deaths of her erring handmaidens, or would her wrath be all the greater because punishment of the Vestals' crimes had been so long delayed? Perhaps the Romans were about to find out, for at this point reports reached the city that the wandering tribes of the Cimbri and Teutones had reached the lands of the Scordisci, right beside the Roman frontier.

It may have seemed at first that the arrival of the Cimbri was actually rather convenient for the Romans. At the time they were engaged in a war against the Scordisci in the mountains northeast of Italy. As the Cimbri moved westward from Illyricum they also bumped into the Scordisci, so that unfortunate tribe was forced to fight a war on two fronts against overwhelmingly powerful enemies. The Scordisci were duly crushed, but passed on to their Cimbric enemies tales of the formidable power of Rome. Accordingly, the Cimbri decided that they would avoid a collision with the Roman war machine by turning northwest and moving through the lands of the Taurisci. (See ending of chapter 1.)

Ironically the Taurisci may well have been near-neighbours of the Cimbri back in the time when both peoples occupied their traditional lands in northwest Europe. The Taurisci seem to have migrated earlier and come to some sort of arrangement with the peoples who were their current neighbours, a tribal confederation called the Norici (who later gave their name to what became the Roman province of Noricum). Doubtless the Taurisci were less than delighted to see the Cimbri again, especially as the Cimbri certainly did not come in peace. In the current clash the Taurisci had one major advantage. Probably because the Romans had wanted to isolate the Scordisci through a series of military pacts, the Taurisci were currently allies of Rome.

The Taurisci accordingly called on the Romans to honour their alliance and the Romans did so, probably because Papirius Carbo, the consul of that year (113 BC), hoped to garner the glory of a victory over a barbarian tribe. Alternatively, if we are to believe the historian Appian, the Romans were merely 'friends' of the Taurisci because as Appian remarks, 'It was the practice of the Romans to make foreign friends of any people for whom they wanted to intervene on the score of friendship, without being obliged to defend them as allies.' (Appian, *Gallic Wars* frags. 1). According to Appian the question was less of honouring a pledge of mutual assistance, and more that the consul was worried that the Cimbri might defeat the Taurisci, cross the alpine passes and enter Italy itself. This was not an unreasonable fear as the nearest Roman city was the colony of Aquelia, near modern Venice, and (according to Strabo) only 1,200 stades (225 kilometres) away from the action. (That Aquelia was so proximate is not really surprising. Like Turin in the west and Milan in the centre, Aquelia in the east was one of the north Italian fortress cities set up by the Romans to control barbarian incursions through the mountain passes.)

There is room for multiple interpretations of this and subsequent events, because the sources for what happened hereafter are horribly obscure. Most Roman historians were interested in writing about the glories of Rome's past, and the early clashes with the Cimbri were anything but glorious. Also, in the late first century we are at a point where the continuous history of Livy breaks down, with the later chapters surviving only as a set of short chapter summaries called the 'Epitomes'. We have Sallust for the near-contemporary Jugurthine War, but otherwise the history of this era has to be picked up in scraps and fragments gleaned from dozens of different texts, epigraphical remains and – to be frank – guesswork. Appian gives us the most complete picture of what happened in Noricum in 113 BC and, though part of his history is definitely suspect, his report is the best we have to go on.

Papirius Carbo, the consul who led Rome's army north, was one of those political generals who epitomized the mediocrity of Roman leadership at this time. (In fact, according to Cicero, the entire clan of the Carbones were far from being an asset to Rome. 'Except for Gaius Carbo ... there has not been one of

the Carbones who ever was a good and useful citizen.') Papirius
Carbo's instructions from the senate allowed him considerable
leeway – he was to investigate the situation with the Taurisci and
thereafter act as he deemed appropriate.

Carbo started by occupying the passes that led into Italy and
waiting there for the Cimbri to come to him. When it became
clear that the Cimbri were not interested in marching on Italy,
Carbo led his men into the lands of the Norici and took the
initiative by attacking the Cimbri (whom Appian at this point
insists on calling the 'Teutones'). When the aggrieved Cimbri (or
Teutones) sent ambassadors asking what they had done to offend
the Romans, Carbo replied that they had attacked a people who
were their friends and allies.

At this time the Cimbric leaders were not interested in butting
heads with the Romans. Their objective was still to find new
lands for their people to occupy. Italy was not currently among the
candidates which the Cimbri considered suitable for settlement,
being occupied by numerous and warlike peoples, not least of
whom were the Romans. (Later, after defeating the Romans on
a regular basis, the Cimbri were to change their minds about
this.) For the moment though, the Cimbri had much to lose and
little to gain by fighting the legions, so they backed down. Their
ambassadors politely informed Carbo that they had been unaware
that the Taurisci and Norici were friends of the Romans. They
would cease hostilities immediately and leave the area by the most
direct route possible.

This led to an immediate outbreak of amity. Carbo helpfully
provided guides who would take the Cimbri out of the lands
of Roman allies, and it was agreed that everyone would part as
friends at the border. Thereafter Carbo told his guides not to take
the Cimbri out of the region by the most direct route possible,
but instead to take the longer path. This allowed Carbo to take
his army at speed along the shorter route to where he had already

picked a spot where his men would fall upon the Cimbri and wipe them out.

This would enrich Carbo with booty and slaves and enhance the military reputation of the Papirii Carbones, all for the price of a broken promise and a little treachery. The potential benefit of such an engagement to Rome itself was slight, since the Cimbri had clearly indicated that they had no wish to fight the Romans and were actively trying to get out of the way. Therefore, Carbo was prepared to antagonize a potentially powerful enemy, diminish even further Rome's already tarnished reputation when it came to broken promises, and risk the lives of the legionaries under his command purely for his personal political and financial gain. Even so, venality and ambition might have been excusable if they were matched with a modicum of military ability – which they were not.

A passing mention by the geographer Strabo gives us the location where the Cimbri and Teutones were intended to meet their doom. This was near Noreia, a fortress-city upon a plateau which was one of the major cities of the northwest (which is why Strabo mentions it). The country hereabouts – near modern Neumarkt in south-central Austria – is woodland with open valleys and gently-sloping, tree-lined hills. It is easy to imagine the mass of the Cimbri moving up one such valley while the legions waited, drawn up secretly on the slopes alongside.

The plan hit an initial snag in that the Cimbri were moving more slowly than Carbo had anticipated. Eventually it became clear that the engagement would take place in the late afternoon. Nevertheless, Carbo remained confident. He ordered the legionaries not to loot the bodies of the fallen Cimbri until dawn on the following day because he believed that otherwise his men would miss some of the gold ornaments with which he was sure the persons of his proposed victims were richly adorned. (*Lexicon of Suidas* in Appian, *frags* 1)

As to what happened next – we have no idea. Livy tells us nothing more than that the Romans were defeated. Strabo says that the Roman ambush 'proved ineffective' and Appian tells us that the army 'suffered severely' for the commander's perfidy, but no-one tells us how Carbo's ambush came so disastrously unglued.

There are several considerations. Firstly, Carbo was no military genius, and deploying legions amid the trees required men who usually fought in close formation to adopt different tactics. Secondly, it is very possible that when the Scordisci warned the Cimbri of Rome's military prowess the topic of the general untrustworthiness of Roman promises also came up, together with the tragic history of those who had recently trusted to Roman good faith. Given such a warning, it would not be hard for the Cimbri to deploy scouts along their line of march to look out for such things as large bodies of Roman troops lurking among the trees. The third alternative is that Carbo had simply underestimated the sheer size of the Cimbric horde (he seems not to have asked himself *why* the Cimbri were moving so slowly) and the Romans therefore charged joyfully downhill only to find themselves enveloped by an army that massively outnumbered their own.

Whatever led to the outcome at Noreia, that outcome was a disaster. Three things prevented it from being an unmitigated disaster. Firstly, fighting broke off because of the lateness of the engagement and secondly because a thunderstorm broke out and many Roman units were able to extricate themselves in the darkness and general confusion. 'The Romans fled through the woods in separate groups and only rallied three days later, and that with difficulty', Appian tells us. That rally was probably at the town of Noreia itself – the presence of a secure rallying point being the third factor that saved Rome from complete disaster.

There was more bad news to come. Although the Cimbri originally claimed that they had killed the Roman commander, it turned out that unfortunately Carbo had survived – unlike hundreds of his men. Nevertheless, the incompetent consul certainly did not escape scot-free from his catastrophic misjudgement. The tribune Marcus Antonius launched a prosecution on behalf of the families who had lost loved ones. Carbo, faced with condemnation and exile, escaped his fate 'by a dose of cobbler's acid' (says Cicero in a throwaway remark in *ad Familiares* 9.21, implying that Carbo committed suicide, though exactly how the acid effected this is uncertain).

Demonstrating yet again how purposeless Carbo's intended ambush had been, the Cimbri showed no interest in following up their victory and entering Italy. Indeed, they did exactly what they would have done had Carbo kept faith with them – they moved away from the territory of Rome and its allies and moved off northwestwards. For a while the Cimbri vanished from the collective Roman consciousness, though doubtless Roman spies kept a keen eye on their movements. (The next time the actual location of the wandering nation appears in the historical record the Cimbri had already crossed the Rhine and entered Gaul. This much we know from Appian, while another writer – Velleius Paterculus – mentions this in conjunction with another unrelated event, which nevertheless gives us a specific date – 106 BC.)

In the meantime, Rome and the Cimbri had certainly not forgotten about each other, but with another round of intense political feuding underway in Rome, and matters not going terribly well in Numidia, contemporary historians neglected to report upon the Cimbri for the benefit of future generations. The tribe were still on the move in 109 BC, as there is a report that they sent ambassadors to the Roman consul who was campaigning somewhere around the river Rhone. The Cimbric argument was that as Rome was the local power it was in the Roman interest to find a suitable place for the Cimbri to settle. In return, the Cimbri were prepared to put their substantial numbers at the disposal of the Roman authorities. The historian Florus, probably drawing upon the lost work of Livy for this period, gives us the Cimbri's own words. 'The children of Mars should give them some land. By way of payment they [the Romans] could put their hands and weapons to any use they wanted.' (Florus, 38.2)

Such agreements did exist in the Republican era, though only for mutual aid through a treaty (*foedus*). What the Cimbri were looking for very much foreshadows the sort of agreement by which some barbarian tribes in the fifth century AD (*foederati*) explicitly traded land for military service.

However, in the Late Roman Empire the state was desperate for men capable of military service. In the Late Republican period the problem was not a manpower shortage but a land shortage – mainly because available land could not be prised out of the grip of the aristocracy. As Florus remarks, the Romans were at that point in the middle of a bitter legislative fight about separating the aristocracy from their substantial landholdings and sharing these with the common people of Rome and Italy. Meanwhile, if even discharged Roman legionaries tended to end up landless, there was no chance whatsoever that the Senate was going to find somewhere to settle a massive and violent horde of climate refugees from northern Germania. The Cimbric request was rejected out of hand.

That a degree of diplomatic contact had taken place was because the Romans and Cimbri had by now taken a long look at each other – and neither had greatly liked what they had seen. From the Roman point of view there were two main issues with the Cimbri – there were a great many of them, and even if that were disregarded, there were a great many more. Plutarch remarks that there were rumoured to be 300,000 'fighting men' and that reality outstripped the rumour. Modern historians tend to regard Roman estimates of enemy numbers with scorn and some historians have eliminated ninety per cent of the Cimbri with a single stroke of the pen.

The fact is that we have no way of really knowing whether the Cimbri numbered in the tens or the hundreds of thousands. However, if they actually numbered 300,000 men, women and children, then even this reduced figure means that the Cimbric nation – apart from their allies – was nearly the same size as the Roman citizen body. (See the census result p.27). The difference was that the Romans had a lot of commitments elsewhere and could only divert a fraction of their manpower to deal with the northern threat, whereas the Cimbri could and did bring every able-bodied male to the battle line.

If the sculptures tentatively identified as Roman depictions of the Cimbri are indeed correct (and these are in line with the warriors illustrated on treasures such as the Gundestrup Cauldron, unearthed from the bogs of Jutland) then the Cimbri were not radically different from the average Germanic warrior whom the Romans faced at this time. Indeed Plutarch (*Marius* 11) remarks 'Most people conjectured that they belonged among the Germanic peoples whose home extends as far as the northern ocean, basing this idea on their great stature and their light-blue eyes.'

Another reason why the Romans thought of the Cimbri as Germanic rather than Celtic was because the Cimbri are described as blond – as were Germans – while contemporary Celts tended towards red or brown hair. That the Cimbri and Teutones were armed and fought in a manner similar to the average German tribesman can be inferred from the fact that if they fought differently to 'other' Germans then the Romans would have commented on the fact. (For example, we know that a distinctive feature of Frankish warfare was their fondness for a throwing axe called the Francesca, and this is mentioned several times by ancient sources.)

Therefore, we can assume that the Cimbric army consisted mainly of warriors fighting on foot. These men were armed with an oblong shield, often with an iron spine and boss, and carried at least a stabbing spear. Those at the fore wore armour, and as time went on that armour was increasingly equipment removed from dead Romans – one advantage of chainmail from the new owner's perspective is that it is relatively easy to re-tailor for a new and larger wearer. The Cimbri in the back ranks were less-well equipped and wore the 'traditional' barbarian dress of boots and a pair of trousers. Fighting bare-chested was not merely a demonstration of macho prowess but also of common sense. In an age before antibiotics, the casualties after a battle could be almost as bad as during the fray itself. Any wound could become infected, but if fibres from a shirt were driven into a wound then infection was much more likely, especially as the chances that the shirt was clean were pretty minimal to start with.

The Romans at least were aware of this problem, and their field dressings included spider webs with which to pack the wound. The Romans did not know that spiderweb contains a natural fungicide, but they did know that spiders did not like their webs going mouldy and had found a way to stop it. They then wrapped the wound in bandages soaked with honey because they had established through empirical observation that this helped to prevent infection. (Which it did, because honey is a low-water solution which leaches moisture from bodies which penetrate it – such as the cells of invading bacteria. These bacteria are having a tough time anyway, because honey is acidic and bacteria thrive in acid-neutral environments, especially those without trace amounts of hydrogen peroxide, which honey also contains.)

Then the Romans would add a protective amulet evoking whatever god the doctor felt might be most effective. This would certainly do no harm and probably helped the patient's mental state.

Probably because of their large numbers the Cimbri chose not to fight in a battle line but in a battle block almost as deep as it was wide. There is considerable dispute among ancient historians as to what effect the literal weight of numbers might have in an ancient battle. Supporters of the 'stand and fight' school assume that deep formations were handy because if a man fell in the front ranks then the man behind him could step up and fight in his place. Also, it is a lot harder to turn and run when one has to elbow through a dozen ranks of one's comrades before routing from the battlefield.

Those behind the 'shove' theory believe that weight had an even more significant role. That is, if you can literally push through the enemy battle line then you are most of the way to breaking the enemy as a fighting force. Therefore, one possible tactic for a block to use against troops in shallow formations is for those in the rear ranks to put their shoulders against the back of the men in front and push them through the enemy ranks like a collective human battering ram.

This technique would be particularly useful for a people such as the Cimbri who were good at fighting as single warriors. The Romans liked to fight in units where every man did his part. Once a unit was broken up, individual Romans were relatively easy prey for the larger, more-agile Cimbri, whose longer swords gave than an advantage in single combat.

On the other hand, when formed battle lines came head-to-head, it was the Romans who had the advantage. This is because the Cimbri liked to use slashing swords which cut through their enemy by their sheer power and velocity. These swords were heavy, up to three feet long and packed substantial kinetic energy. Some did not even have a sharpened tip, because the wielder was unlikely to do much sustained fencing with several pounds of steel at arm's length. While devastating in individual combat, those swinging such swords needed a goodly amount of space in which to work, lest the wielder decapitate the warriors on each side of him. This made fighting in close formation problematic, for re-enactments have shown that even a careful user of a slashing sword needs around four feet of space before he is less of a menace to his fellow combatants than he is to the enemy.

The Romans (and those allies who were equipped and trained in the same manner) had several advantages so long as they stayed in formation. Firstly, the Romans had been fighting wild barbarian tribes from the north for centuries, and to some extent their weapons, armour and tactics had evolved to meet the threat.

(We should note yet again that 'barbarian' is a purely Roman designation for these opponents. In terms of weaponry, Gallic swords and armour were every bit as well manufactured as the Roman – perhaps better as the Romans were probably mass manufacturing swords even at this point, whereas each 'barbarian' sword was craftsman-produced. The difference between the two sides was one of tactics rather than technology.)

The Roman army was at this time in a process of evolution, having gone from a phalanx-style battle formation in the style of the ancient Greeks to one of smaller, more-manoeuvrable units – partly as a result of clashes with tribesmen from Spain, where the locals preferred hit-and-run actions in small groups against which a formed battle line was useless. The Romans discovered that it was better to fight with handfuls of men who could be united into a larger block if required.

The historian Polybius – a military man himself – described the Roman formations in detail. His description dates back to the Punic Wars of a century previously, but it seems that little had changed thereafter. Roman military formations of the early stages of the Cimbric wars were already overdue for updating and reform. The 'small handfuls' of men were literally called that – 'maniples' – and each contained around 120 legionaries. In a maniple formed up for battle, at the fore were skirmishers called *velites*, because the Romans had realized that heavy troops alone are ineffective against lighter armed opponents who can simply skip aside from their cumbersome charge. However, when *velites* were added to the formation, light troops opposing them had the unenviable options of turning their backs to run, thus exposing their backs to the *velites*, or standing (briefly) against a heavy infantry charge.

Velites were generally the poorest class of infantryman. At this time Roman soldiers needed to purchase their own armour and weaponry, and *velite* gear was cheaper than legionary kit. It consisted of a throwing spear and a small, round shield called a parma. *Velites* were often shown as wearing wolfskin caps to differentiate them from the enemy in what was often a confused melee situation, but it is unknown whether this was a universal practice.

The men in the line of formed infantry directly behind the *velites* were the *hastati*, or literally 'spearmen'. *Hastati* were generally younger or poorer soldiers who might wear a bronze breastplate instead of the increasingly popular chainmail. They carried a short stabbing sword (*gladius*) and two spears (*pila*). The *pilum* was a heavy throwing spear which was hurled at the enemy immediately before the fighting got up close and personal.

The *pilum* differed from the average spear in that it had a long iron shank which finished in a small pyramidal head. All the velocity of a well-flung *pilum* was concentrated into that small tip at the moment of impact, and the effect was often enough to propel the tip through a shield and into the person sheltering behind it. Even if full penetration was not achieved, a *pilum* coming through a shield was generally an indication that there was a legionary arriving close behind it. Therefore there was little time to remove the *pilum* for effective shield use, even if the iron shank had not bent and further hindered removal. There is some debate as to whether this bending shank was a bug or a feature, for, although it certainly handicapped the enemy in combat, the Romans had to retrieve and attempt to straighten the things afterwards. This was a fiddly and time-consuming task which makes no sense to deliberately take on for something that provided little extra benefit in combat.

Armed and equipped as they were, the *hastati* were thus trained heavy infantrymen capable of defeating many tribal units on their own. In a more serious battle, their task was to blunt the force of an enemy attack, or cripple an enemy defence. Thereafter the battle could be finished off by the principal arm of the Roman killing machine, which consisted of units called, naturally enough, the *principes*.

Apart from being more likely to sport chainmail, *principes* were armed and equipped in a like manner to the *hastati*. The main difference was that the *principes* were veteran soldiers usually in their mid-twenties to late thirties. Being generally the heads of their own households, *principes* could usually afford better-made weaponry and they were also more-experienced fighters. Generally, their success or failure would determine the outcome of a hard-fought battle.

That said, if the *principes* did fail, there was a third and final line of defence. A beaten Roman army could still fall back in good order behind a line of spearmen called the *triarii*. While long spears were not as useful as heavy throwing spears or stabbing swords for offensive manoeuvres, that was not the point of this unit. The *triarii* were experienced veterans who were less inclined to panic when things were not going their way. Their spears were designed to keep the enemy in front of an organized battle line while the *hastati* and *principes* re-organized behind them.

If a battle reached the point where the *triarii* were needed then this was the make-or-break point where a retreat could turn into a rout. In fact, this was the point of the contemporary Roman saying that things had 'come to the *triarii*' – meaning that matters were desperate but salvageable.

In terms of armour, apart from the fact that theirs was generally the best that could be obtained, *triarii* were kitted out as were their fellow legionaries. The standard helmet of this period was the so-called Montefortino type. This was more conical than the helmets of later centuries and designed to deflect a downward-slashing sword from the wearer's skull to his shoulders, which were thickly padded with chainmail for this eventuality.

There are suggestions that the *triarii* had longer plumes in their helmets. This was for psychological effect, for the *triarii* spent the first part of a battle relaxing on one knee while the fighting went on in front of them. Then, if the first two ranks had to retreat, the advancing, and presumably already-somewhat-battered enemy would be confronted by a line of tall shapes rising as if from the earth to meet the enemy with an unyielding wall of spears.

Shields were designed also to blunt the force of a furious initial assault. At this time the infantry shield was an elongated oval – though truncated ends were becoming popular. The shield was of plywood with each layer laid at right angles to the previous layer, so that the wood could not be split along the grain. A metal spine called an umbo was fitted to the middle, with a boss by which the shield was grasped on the user's side. This boss gave the shield offensive potential as it could be punched into the face of an enemy while that enemy's defensive reaction allowed greater freedom for the insertion of the legionary's main killing weapon – a short stabbing sword called the *gladius hispaniensis*.

That the Roman helmet (*galea*) and chain mail are Gallic in origin while the sword was modelled on a Spanish prototype shows that not only was Roman military technology no better than that of their enemies – it was often copied from them. Unlike their northern enemies who preferred edge weapons for close combat, the point of the *gladius* was, well, the point. The Roman sword was designed to be thrust straight out with minimal lateral movement. There was not much room for lateral movement anyway as when in formation the Romans fought almost literally shoulder-to-shoulder.

This closeness in close combat meant that individual Romans needed only three feet of space to the enemy's minimum of four. Therefore, no matter how many barbarians were massed against a Roman army, at the cutting edge the Romans outnumbered the enemy four-to-three. In fact, the odds were slightly better than that, because the Romans practised drill while their enemies practised swordsmanship. Swinging several pounds of steel is hard work, especially under stressful circumstances, and even the best-trained fighter cannot keep it up for long. A well-drilled Roman was able to step back from the front lines when he was tired or wounded, while his opponent was likely to fight until he literally dropped.

The same applied to Roman units, where *velites* could fall back past *hastati*, who could drop back past the *principes* and everyone could re-organize behind the *triarii* if it came to that. By comparison, it seems that the favoured tactic of the Cimbri was to put the best warriors at the front and hit the enemy as a sort of human tidal wave that rolled unstoppably over the more elaborate infantry formations. If the mass of the Cimbri were slowed, their huge numbers would simply flow around the sides of an opposing formation until they reached an exposed flank and tore the enemy apart from there.

When a collapse did happen, the Cimbri were ready to follow up with cavalry. Most casualties on an ancient battlefield did not happen while well-armoured battle lines came together, but when one or the other line collapsed into rout, and the victors were able to run down and kill almost-defenceless opponents as they fled. Here, of course, horsemen had it all their own way, and one of the main purposes of ancient cavalry was simply to massacre as much of a broken army as possible.

Cavalry were also used for scouting, interdicting supply chains and for driving around the flank of a battle line – often by clearing away the cavalry of the enemy who had the same intentions.

The Cimbric cavalry were particularly formidable, though their numbers were small relative to the rest of the army. According to Plutarch:

> the horsemen ... rode out in splendid style, with helmets made as though they were terrifying wild animals with gaping jaws or the heads of strange beasts. These, together with tall crests made of feathers, made the riders seem much taller than they were. Each man had an iron breastplate and a white shield. They carried two throwing spears and had long heavy swords for close combat. (Plutarch, *Marius* 25)

Thus we can imagine early Romano-Cimbric clashes on the battlefield as Roman military sophistication and technique against Cimbric brute force and numbers. In the early years brute force and numbers won every time, not least because the mediocre commanders whom Roman politics had put in command of their armies were unable to use their troops to their full potential. Also, military formations optimized to defeat similarly sized or smaller units were unable to deal with the massive blocks of Cimbric warriors. Against an enemy who attacked with such overwhelming force the Roman army was not fit for purpose. It would take tens of thousands of deaths before Roman pragmatism won over Roman stubbornness and the army was reformed.

Chapter 4

The Road to Arausio

One might assume that, having been given a solid kicking by a barbarian army at Noreia, the Roman response would be to plunge right back into the fray to avenge the honour of the Republic. This did not happen. A cynic might suggest that this was because the Roman Republic of the late second century BC did not have a lot of honour to avenge anyway. More realistically though, in terms of foreign and military policy at this time, the Romans had a great deal going on and they were not on top of very much of it. Now that the Cimbri had moved northwestwards out of the Roman sphere of influence the Romans were happy to ignore them and focus on more-pressing problems.

For a start they had two other military issues on hand. The Romans needed urgently to calm the situation in northeast Italy where the Boii and the recently quashed Scordisci remained resentful threats, along with the wasp's nest of Illyria which the Cimbri had so recently kicked over. This impending crisis alone was excuse enough to ignore the departing Cimbri but secondly, and more importantly, there was the matter of the very annoying Jugurtha of Numidia.

It did not escape the Roman people that Jugurtha had killed Italians, blatantly ignored the demands of the Senate, brutally murdered his brother while that man was under Roman protection, and violated every treaty he had ever signed. For all of which he had been allowed to take over his father's kingdom for the price of a trivial fine. This exercised political debate in Rome much more than the fallout of the Battle of Noreia, which after Carbo's death was quickly dismissed as a defeat by a mediocre commander against an unknown tribe somewhere obscure beyond Rome's borders. What the Roman public now demanded to know was exactly why Jugurtha had got off so lightly for his crimes, and whom he had paid for his good fortune.

The people were angry with Jugurtha, but incensed with their own leaders. A tribune called Memmius made this his special cause and repeatedly hammered away at the 'cruelty, inefficiency and deep corruption' of the ruling class. (Says Sallust, *Jugurthine War* 28 *passim*) In attacking the aristocracy in this way Memmius was doing a tribune's job, for the office had been created in a period of particularly stressful civil unrest several centuries before. Among the concessions made by the aristocracy was the creation of tribunes, who could only be plebeians and who were supposed to hold the aristocracy to account. For this purpose, tribunes had extensive and wide-ranging powers which had been used to good purpose by, for instance, the reforming Gracchus brothers.

However, as the highly-bred Gracchi demonstrate, by the second century the Roman aristocracy was as much plebeian as it was patrician, and aristocratic tribunes could use their powers to twist the political process for their own ends. Nevertheless, as well as political hacks from the nobility, the system still produced crusading tribunes such as Memmius, and Memmius had the wind of popular opinion behind him. Eventually the establishment were forced into agreeing to a commission that would enquire as to the circumstances leading to the farcical end of the Numidian War. The witness whom everyone most wanted to hear from was Jugurtha but Jugurtha was, not unnaturally, leery of presenting himself in the middle of the very city which he had offended so deeply. Jugurtha eventually agreed to come, his presence aided by a promise that whatever the result of the enquiry, he would be allowed to leave unhindered.

The promise of immunity was not Jugurtha's main incentive. His main reason for coming to Rome was to deflect the warlike tendencies of the consul-elect for 110 BC, who was a man called Albinus. Albinus was from a minor political family, and was eager for glory and loot and reasonably sure that a war with Jugurtha would supply both. If Jugurtha refused to testify then Albinus had announced that he was ready, willing and eager to lead an army to Africa and place another member of the royal line on the Numidian throne. This member was a man called Massiva, who had earlier drawn the correct conclusions from the fate of the rest of his family and fled from Jugurtha's clutches to sanctuary in Rome.

The day of Jugurtha's testimony came, and the renegade king presented himself – only to have a tribune called Baebius rise and forbid Jugurtha from speaking. Since one of the fundamental principles of Roman governance was that a veto always over-ruled an action, there was nothing the fuming Memmius could do to force Jugurtha to testify. No-one doubted for a second that Baebius had been bribed, and bribed so substantially that he was prepared to risk the outrage of the people, the end of his political career and, presumably, some degree of self-reproach for shamelessly prostituting himself in this manner.

Nevertheless, the trip to Rome was not a complete waste of time from Jugurtha's point of view. While there, he was able to make in person the arrangements for the assassination of his rival Massiva, and in so doing demonstrate once again his massive contempt for the Roman political establishment. Nor did Jugurtha even bother to disguise his complicity in the assassination, for after all, he had come to Rome with a promise of immunity – and this was a promise that it was in the interest of the aristocracy to keep. All the frustrated Memmius could do was ensure that Jugurtha was expelled from Rome at once, and then persuade Albinus to persevere with his planned war against Jugurtha, even though the only suitable replacement king was now deceased.

It is said that as Jugurtha was leaving Rome he turned back in the saddle for one last look and remarked in disgust, 'A city for sale, and doomed if it ever finds a buyer.'

War was now inevitable, not least because Romans of a thoughtful disposition could see that the Cimbri may well again appear on Rome's borders at any time. Therefore, dealing with Jugurtha while the Cimbri were away would mean that when the Cimbri returned – as they probably would – Rome could dedicate a considerably greater proportion of the city's military might to dealing with the northern problem.

While the situation in Numidia had now become more urgent, Jugurtha's trip to Rome for his non-testimony had succeeded in delaying the commencement of Albinus' African war. The result was that Albinus had barely succeeded in getting his campaign off the ground before he was compelled, as consul, to return from Africa to Rome to oversee the next year's elections there. In the hope that his command would be promulgated for the following year so that he could campaign in Africa as a proconsul, Albinus handed over the army to his brother Aulus.

Albinus was a mediocre commander, but Aulus was a very bad one. (In fact he was so uninspiring a leader that in a later war he was eventually murdered by his own men.) While Albinus had asked only that Aulus act as a sort of human bookmark to keep his place until he could return to the campaign, Aulus had other ideas. The ambition of Aulus was further fuelled by the fact that the elections in Rome that year were severely delayed by two bickering tribunes and this kept Albinus from returning to his troops for much longer than planned.

With Aulus in charge, morale in the army went downhill like a runaway train. The men were enervated by idleness and demoralized by incompetent leadership, and all the while the envoys of Jugurtha went secretly about the camp purchasing the loyalty of officers and men. Encouraged by his brother's prolonged absence, Aulus decided to take independent action and strike at the town of Suthul, not because the place had any great strategic value but because it contained Jugurtha's treasury. After all, why take money from the king when one could bypass the distributor and go directly to the source?

Needless to say, the attempt was a disaster so complete that Aulus ended up surrendering himself and his entire army to the Numidians. In surrendering, Aulus did perhaps the only sensible thing he ever did as a military commander, for the alternative was fighting to the death with an army that was already doomed by poor morale, enemy infiltration and poor generalship. At least by a humiliating surrender Aulus was able to save the lives of men that the Romans were going to need later when the Cimbri returned.

Also, in surrendering Aulus placed the initiative firmly with Jugurtha. Jugurtha knew that he had already pushed Roman patience well beyond its limits, and massacring or enslaving an army of captured Romans was something that Rome would never forgive. If Jugurtha went down that road then he would irrevocably commit his country to a war with Rome that would end only when one or the other nation was completely destroyed. Decadent and corrupt as Rome might be, the city had a reputation for holding grudges for centuries if necessary, as the Carthaginians and Macedonians, among others, could testify – if they were only still around to do so.

So Jugurtha extracted from Aulus a peace settlement mild enough that he hoped that the Senate in Rome would ratify it and released Rome's captive army. However, his pride forced him into a major misstep, for Jugurtha wanted to be one of the few commanders in history to make a Roman army pass under the yoke. 'Passing under the yoke' was a particularly humiliating acknowledgement of defeat by which disarmed soldiers had to bend under a low bar, showing their buttocks to an enemy who mocked them from the sidelines. While this was preferable to wholesale massacre, an army forced to submit in this way was so disgraced that morale was unlikely to ever recover. Sallust sums up the result.

> An army of weak cowards, as incapable of facing hardship as they were of facing danger. … capable only of robbing their friends while being victimized by the enemy, and at once undisciplined and out of hand. Any new commander was more likely to worry about how many useless bodies he had to cure of bad habits than he was to be reassured that the size of his army offered any hope of success. (Sallust, *Jugurthine War* 44ff)

In Rome the news of defeat in Africa, following as it did the equally severe, though less humiliating, defeat by the Cimbri of Carbo in Noricum, roused the voters to a pitch of incandescent fury. Despite desperate attempts by the guilty parties to pull the levers of power from behind the scenes, nothing would deter the voters but to see the principal actors in the Numidian debacle hauled before a commission of enquiry, humiliated, fined and exiled.

After that the Romans did what they should have done in the first place and elected someone suitable to do the job. This was Quintus Caecilius Metellus, a Roman of the old school – stiff-necked and incorruptible, and an uninspired but very competent commander. Metellus could be relied upon to ignore Jugurtha's blandishments while he grimly and methodically brought the Numidians to heel.

With Africa finally being handled by a competent general, it fell to the other consul, Junius Silanus, to stabilize matters in the north. The Cimbri might still be beyond Rome's frontiers, but the migrant barbarian tribe remained an active threat.

Because the attention of Roman historians was firmly fixed on Africa, events in the north are obscure even for the late second century – a period in Roman history infamous for its obscurity. Events are mentioned in passing and usually as an aside to something which those making the passing reference consider more important. Nor does it help that Rome's history with the Cimbri is up to this point an embarrassing catalogue of misjudgement and incompetence which in later years most patriotic Romans were only too happy to forget.

Marcus Junius Silanus is himself a relatively obscure figure, though his family was to rise to greater prominence in the Late Republic. His family were plebeian and either Silanus or a relative had been Tribune of the Plebs in 124 or 123 BC. Also, there are suggestions that Silanus might before then have been director of the national mint and been involved with legislation limiting the reasons why a man might be excused from the annual levy for military service. Apart from the latter legislation, there is no suggestion that Silanus was a military man or that he came from a family with a military background. Given that his opponents were the by-now-comprehensively battle-hardened Cimbri, the outcome of any clash was somewhat predictable.

According to one account, the Romans and Cimbri clashed when the Cimbri, unable to force their way into Gaul, tried to move into Italy instead. Having had their overtures for a peaceful land settlement rejected, they turned on Silanus and his army in order to take what they wanted by force. This account comes from the historian Florus (*Epitome* 38) and was written two hundred years after the events it describes. Regrettably for a historian whose work is intended as a summary of Rome's wars, Florus omits some crucial details, such as when the clash with Silanus took place and the size of the armies involved. The one detail he does provide is that the Cimbri 'Descended [through the passes] into Italy' and this is highly suspect since a battle fought on the Italian side of the Alps would have received a lot more attention from contemporary historians.

Our best source for events in the late second century is Livy, a near-contemporary historian, but his history of events exists only as a later, highly condensed summary. So, from Livy we know that 'the consul Marcus Julius Silanus fought without success against the Cimbri' (*Epitome* 65). Florus tells us that he was defeated and his camp captured and the early imperial historian Velleius Paterculus adds that his army was scattered (*History* 2.12). Annoyingly, all of these sources describe only the upshot of Silanus' campaign, without giving any details of what led up to this unhappy outcome. Cicero adds the information that Silanus was later prosecuted for his poor conduct of the war, but he was acquitted. No explanation of the charges or the reason for the acquittal have come down to posterity

None of these sources say where this confrontation took place, so, if we politely ignore Florus, a reasonable guess would put the clash somewhere on the boundaries of Transalpine Gaul. While all of the sources here describe the clash as a comprehensive defeat for Rome, evidently the Cimbri also found it a bruising experience. Thereafter, as they had done after the battle with Carbo at Noreia, they once again moved out of range of the Romans and disappeared from history for several years. This makes a suitably obscure end to a campaign so poorly documented that one can only observe that it happened and the Romans lost, and then move on from there.

The focus now returns to North Africa, not so much because Metellus was slowly but successfully grinding down Jugurtha but more because of the rise of Metellus' second-in-command. This subordinate was a man called Caius Marius, whose relatively humble origins were overshadowed by his ambition and his determination to realize those ambitions whatever the cost (to others). This Marius was the man who was later to lead Rome's armies in the climactic confrontation with the Cimbri, so it is worth following his earlier career to that point.

While most sources for the Cimbric wars are late, confused and obscure, we are fortunate to have the complete *Life of Marius* by the biographer Plutarch. This text takes readers all the way from Marius' birth in Arpinum to poor parents (Plutarch cites highly improbable reports that they were manual labourers) all the way to his ignominious death in 86 BC, long after the Cimbric wars had ended. Unlike the unfortunate Silanus, Marius was very much a military man. While young, he had served in the Spanish wars and earned high praise from Scipio Aemilianus, who was perhaps the greatest general of his day.

After the war, Marius sought political office in Rome and found it tough going. As a rustic outsider he lacked the money, connections and sophistication to easily participate in the dinners and social events at which many of the affairs of Rome were decided behind the scenes. Realizing that he would never be accepted by the powerbrokers of the aristocracy, Marius instead took a '*popularis*' stance and presented himself as a man of the people who stood up to a corrupt and decadent Senate. While this probably saved his political career, it also alienated Marius from the very men who had supported him thus far. It also caused a rift with the Metelli who had been traditional patrons of the Marian family – which is another indication that the family of Marius were far from the humble peasants that later legend made them out to be.

However, Marius was nothing if not persistent, and repeated attempts to get elected earned him enough name-recognition for him to be eventually appointed praetor. This boosted his standing to the point where he was able to make an advantageous match with an aristocratic family of great antiquity which was rising from a long period of decline to become a force in Roman politics. This was the clan of the Julii Caesares – and in fact Marius' bride was later to become the aunt to that Caesar, J., who was assassinated on the Ides of March in 44 BC.

With this extra boost to his respectability and because
Metellus needed someone popular with the people to help
with public support for his African war, Marius was chosen as
Metellus' legate (i.e. second-in-command). Plutarch remarks
that most people would have felt indebted to the person who had
given their career such a boost, but apparently Marius felt that
he owed his promotion to the power of Fortune rather than to
Caecilius Metellus. Therefore, Marius felt no compunction about
undermining his commander for the cause of the greater glory of
Caius Marius and for the potentially greater opportunities that
his current position offered him.

Firstly then, Marius worked hard to undermine his commander
and simultaneously endear himself to the soldiers – who were also
voters with families which voted back in Rome.

> The Roman soldier considers it most agreeable to see his
> general eating bread in the common mess, sleeping on a
> soldier's bed and joining in with the construction of a wall
> or a ditch. While they admire those commanders who
> share honour and booty with them they even more admire
> those who endure the same labour and risks as themselves.
> … Marius won the hearts of his soldiers by doing all this
> and more. … Men in the camp wrote home that the only
> way to finish the war would be to choose Marius as consul.
> (Plutarch, *Marius* 7)

When Marius did ask Metellus for permission to leave his post
to stand for the consulship, Metellus proposed that Marius wait
until later, when he could campaign in tandem with Metellus' son.
This suggestion was less than helpful, for the younger Metellus
was little more than a boy at this time. (He was later to grow up
to become a dedicated enemy of Marius.) This cool response to
the request of Marius shows that Metellus, like the competent

commander that he was, was well aware of what Marius was doing with the army and why.

Yet, while Marius and Metellus did not get along, Metellus helped both Marius and Rome in one highly significant way. Serving under Metellus meant Marius had the rare experience for a contemporary Roman of serving under two very competent commanders – Scipio Aemilianus and Metellus. As a result, Marius learned at first-hand how a Roman army should be handled, and also the many limitations to what that army could do. While commanders such as Metellus were too hide-bound by tradition to make necessary changes, doubtless Marius spent much of his time in Africa noting things he would change should he be given the chance. It also helped that his chosen tactic of talking to the common soldiery gave him an idea of what things the men doing the actual fighting thought might be improved. Overall, Africa was an essential learning experience for him.

In 107 BC, Marius did stand successfully for the consulship and did so on a platform based on the claim that Metellus was deliberately dragging out the war for his own purposes. If the Romans wanted to see their army return home any time soon, claimed Marian propagandists, then the people should elect Marius as commander to finish Jugurtha once and for all. (Many historians reckon that Marius was able to make such a bold claim because as a serving officer in Africa he was well aware that Metellus had already pushed Jugurtha to the brink of defeat.)

Once elected, Marius immediately instituted the first of what were to be many radical changes to the Roman army. This first step was to make enrolment into the legions open to any Roman citizen. Previously, as was normal in the ancient world, enlistment in the main body of the army had been restricted to those who met a certain property qualification. Yet Marius needed men for the strategy he planned to use against Jugurtha and, thanks to changes in Roman land-holding (as discussed in earlier chapters), the numbers of the peasantry who had heretofore supplied the backbone of the legions were in steep decline.

Enrolling landless men was a short-term solution which solved the Roman army's immediate manpower problem while banking greater trouble for the future. That the army was only open to land-holders in antiquity was not because ancient generals were fond of keeping their armies small. It was because those who owned land were stakeholders in the establishment and could therefore be counted upon to fight for the status quo.

Giving military training to men who had nothing to lose and plenty to gain from overturning the system was considered a recipe for, well, the sort of unrest that was to plague the Roman Republic for the remainder of its days. It became expected that once a general had led his men on campaign for several years (as Rome waged wars ever further afield, commands and periods of service alike became extended), then when the general and his men returned home that general would find land on which to settle his veterans, who would thereafter be more loyal to their former commander than to Rome itself. This system was to lead to several failed coups and the general chaos of the final years of the Republic.

For now though, Marius had a large army to lead in Africa and enough men left over for his fellow consul, a man called Cassius Longinus, to take another army to control a potential crisis developing in the north. Longinus had two major issues to deal with. The first was, of course, the threat of the huge Cimbric army which was still hovering over the Roman Republic like a vulture over a wounded buffalo. The other issue was that Rome's string of defeats had not gone unnoticed among the native tribes of the region, where Rome's reputation for military prowess had taken a severe hit. Several Gallic and Helveti peoples were now considering allying with the Cimbri against Rome, which would have made Longinus' job of keeping the peace in the northwest all the more difficult.

While we have Sallust and Plutarch to keep track of events in Africa, the record of events north of the Alps has survived mostly in the works of Orosius, a historian writing half a millennium later. Orosius was an evangelical Christian whose purpose in writing history was mainly to promote the greater glory of God, but nevertheless he had access to earlier, less polemical records from the pagan era which are now lost. From the few paragraphs in which he discusses Longinus in the north (Orosius, *History*, 5.22ff) and scraps from elsewhere, we can reconstruct something of the northern campaign of 107 BC.

It is uncertain where the Cimbric host was at this point, though a good guess might place them on the banks of the Rhone, not far from the territory of the Gallic tribe of the Aedui. Longinus and his army were headed in this general direction, less to take on the Cimbri head-on than to deal with a Helveti tribe called the Tigurini. This tribe, which seems to have its origins in the region around modern Zurich, had allied itself with the Cimbri and in 109 BC had moved west into Gaul for a massive raid which had Rome's allies in the region urgently demanding protection.

Longinus was ready and willing to provide such protection, and able also, if Orosius is to be credited, for he claims that 'The consul Cassius [Longinus] went to Gaul and chased the Tigurini as far as Ocean [the Atlantic]'. This suggests a heady chase indeed, though it is improbable that it went right across what was later to become the Roman territory of Gaul. There seems no reason to doubt though, that the Tigurini were none too eager to engage with what was still a formidable Roman fighting machine. The two forces clashed near Tolosa (modern Toulouse) but exactly when this happened in the course of the campaign is uncertain.

It is clear that the main concern of the Tigurini was to keep out of Longinus' way, which they could do because they were more mobile – they were raiders after all and their interest was in booty rather than battle. Also, the Tigurini did not have the long, cumbersome baggage trains which were a feature of contemporary Roman armies. Therefore, the raiders had little trouble avoiding battle until Longinus gave up the chase.

Believing that the Tigurini had little taste for battle made Longinus careless, and in returning to Roman territory he appears not to have bothered to use scouts to check his route. This led to a catastrophe somewhere in Gaul. Connoisseurs of Roman military disasters can pick a location for the battle depending upon whether they follow Livy (who gives Nitiobriges in modern Aquitania), Caesar (near Lyon) or Orosius (Burdigala/Bordeaux). There are suggestions that the Tigurini had at this point linked up with elements of the Cimbri or Teutones and these, with the memory of Carbo's failed ambush in near Noreia in mind, had decided to show the Romans how such ambushes were done properly.

As mentioned earlier, the Roman ability to conquer huge numbers of barbarian enemies was largely due to the Romans fighting in close-packed, highly organized formations. When, while still in column of march, they were hit with a broadside of barbarians charging out of the woods, the legionaries were largely helpless. Before they could get into battle formation they were surrounded and massacred. Longinus paid for his complacence with his life and along with him fell his second-in-command, a man called Lucius Piso. (We know of the latter because he was the grandfather of Caesar's father-in-law, and Caesar took great pleasure in avenging the man's death when he defeated the Helveti at the start of his Gallic campaigns.)

A good proportion of the Roman army survived, though it is uncertain whether they fought their way out of the trap or were never caught in it in the first place, being on detached duty elsewhere. Orosius adds that survivors of the ambush also fled to the Roman camp (possibly the marching camp which a Roman army constructed at the end of each day on the move). This left C. Popilius Laenas, the most senior surviving Roman commander, in an invidious position. His men had a temporary fort in which they could hold out for a while, but they were deep in foreign territory with no prospect of help and surrounded by barbarian hordes. The choices were between surrender and an inglorious death, so Laenas accordingly set out to explore what offers of surrender the Tigurini and their allies would accept.

For the second time in a decade an enemy leader had to decide what to do with a Roman army that he had completely at his mercy. This time, passing the captured Romans under the yoke was a good idea because it further demolished Rome's crumbling military reputation in the region. Furthermore, the surrender terms meant that the Romans had to give up half their property which, because it was handed over in an orderly fashion, probably amounted to more than the disorganized sack of a captured camp would have yielded. Finally, the Tigurini won almost everything they wanted from a victory without actually having to fight a Roman force which was this time ready and waiting and which had nothing to lose.

Therefore, surrender followed by passing under the yoke is what seems to have happened. 'Seems' because apart from common agreement that the surrender agreement was 'disgraceful' (Orosius' choice of word) everyone writing later histories was too embarrassed to say exactly what the Romans gave up. Appian mentions passing under the yoke, and Orosius adds that the Romans also had to give up hostages. Detailed discussion of the event is, perhaps understandably, unavailable.

This humiliation in the north was a bitter contrast to the news from Africa, where Marius had – after unexpectedly hard fighting – largely brought Numidia under Roman control. Since Longinus had already paid the price of incompetence, the wrath of the Roman people fell upon the unfortunate Laenas, who was brought to trial for 'giving up Roman hostages' (confirms Cicero in a passing reference). Exactly what Laenas was meant to have done differently other than allowing the pointless deaths of the legionaries under his command was unclear, so he was essentially punished for being on the losing side. In 106 BC he was brought to trial and forced into exile.

There was also a sentiment among the Romans that the crisis in the north had gone on for too long already. With the Jugurthine War reaching a conclusion, it was time for Rome to turn its full military might upon the Cimbri and deal with the threat once and for all. Once Jugurtha had been dealt with, the Romans could deploy their full military might to the north. However great their numbers, the Cimbri could never stand against two consular Roman armies in full battle array. Could they?

Chapter 5

Disaster

Consular elections in Rome were always a fraught political struggle. Different factions each promoted their favoured candidate, often with the help of extensive bribery and an increasing degree of violence. There were hastily-arranged and shifting alliances, and a considerable amount of horse-trading went on behind the scenes. Generally, the aristocracy could rely on getting at least one of their number elected because Rome's 'democracy' was deeply skewed in their favour.

The electoral body which chose the consuls for the coming year was the *comitia centuriata*, and for most of its existence this was basically the Roman army in togas. As with the Roman army, the basic unit of voters in the *comitia centuriata* was the century (which as with the Roman army, did not contain the hundred men that the name implies). The voting in a century worked in the same way as votes in a modern constituency – that is, even if the votes split almost down the middle, the majority vote of a particular century counted as that century's entire vote. The centuries voted in turn and the majority vote of the centuries decided an election. So if a majority was reached early, the rest of the voters went home without casting a ballot.

While the actual arrangements of the assembly were somewhat arcane, the basic idea was that the more equipment a man could bring to war, the more voting power he possessed. Women did not fight and thus did not vote. (The Romans were relatively enlightened when it came to the treatment of women but came nowhere near close to equality.) To the Romans it made sense that in a consular election the army should be doing the voting because the consuls whom the soldiers appointed would be the state's war-leaders in the year's forthcoming campaigns.

Power was mostly in the hands of the wealthy because they could supply cavalry horses as well as their own well-armoured selves. Therefore, there were fewer of them in a century than there were common infantrymen in each of the centuries which voted later. Since every century's vote counted equally, the fewer men there were in a century, the more power each voter had. At the very bottom of the heap were the *caput censi* – those numbered by head-count rather than by property valuation. These were all lumped into a single century, which voted last, if at all.

Voting order was also important because the smaller centuries of wealthy voters went first, and were generally well on the way towards establishing a consensus before the second class centuries voted. By the time the centuries of common infantryman got a vote only a few dozen centuries generally need cast their ballots before a majority was reached, and voting on a candidate was closed.

To further skew the balance towards the aristocracy, voting had to be done in Rome in person. This meant that those centuries made of up 'tribes' (the thirty-five voting blocs into which Roman voters were further divided) further from Rome were more thinly manned. Those who actually came to Rome for the voting were generally the richer members of the tribe who could afford to leave their land outside Rome for long enough to travel to the capital, and naturally these voters tended to favour the aristocracy. The most densely-packed centuries belonged to the urban tribes of the city of Rome itself, and many of the voters here were clients of the wealthy, who instructed them how to vote and bribed those whom they could not threaten.

Finally, the Romans themselves were a thoroughly conservative people with an ingrained (though currently fast-fading) respect for their 'betters'. As believers in eugenics millennia before the term was invented, the Romans were keen believers in the particular qualities of various aristocratic bloodlines. If it was felt that Rome needed a general the voters selected a Scipio, while if legal reforms were required one selected a Scaevola, and so on. Furthermore, in a society where forms of communication were few and primitive, name recognition counted for a lot and some of the top families had been supplying Rome with consuls for generations.

For the election of the consuls of 105 BC there were several factors which broke the usual lock which the aristocracy kept on these occasions. Firstly, there was the success of Marius in Africa. – Marius was a *novus homo* or 'new man', as the Romans referred to those who were the first in their families to gain consular office. His election had resulted in military success for Rome, while the aristocratic consul of the same year, L. Cassius Longinus, had gone down to disgraceful defeat at the hands of the Tigurini.

In this, the final year of the African war against Jugurtha, Marius had driven the renegade king from his Numidian homeland to take refuge with his father-in-law, King Bocchus of Mauritania. To persuade Bocchus to give up his guest, Marius sent a senior officer on a risky mission to the Mauritanian royal court. This senior officer was a man called Sulla whom Marius already considered a potential rival, and whose loss would cause him to shed no tears. Sulla succeeded brilliantly, and once Jugurtha had been surrendered to Rome, Marius' prestige rose dramatically. In the following election campaign Marius supported a man called Mallius Maximus, and he used his current popularity to launch relentless attacks alleging corruption and incompetence in the aristocracy – allegations which the aristocracy sometimes seemed to go out of their way to prove. These attacks wore down the confidence of Romans in their traditional leaders even as they showed the Romans that alternatives were available.

Therefore, in the end neither of the consuls who emerged from the electoral struggle were from the aristocratic families which were accustomed to winning consulships. Instead, the winners were the first in their families to become consul, C. Mallius Maximus and P. Rutilius Rufus.

Exactly why Mallius had gained the cognomen of 'Maximus' ('the greatest') is unknown since the man was mediocre at best. (Cicero in *Pro Plancio* 12 calls him 'not just a nonentity, but a worthless, unintelligent one.') His main appeal to the voters was what he was not – that is, he was not from an established family and nor was he a straw man controlled by them. So far as can be determined, he was a member of the fast-growing pro-Marius faction in the Senate, and was indebted to Marius for the endorsement which had helped to push him to victory.

Like Mallius, Rutilius Rufus was a *novus homo*, but hardly an unknown quality since the clan of the Rutilii had been active in Roman politics for at least two generations. Rufus himself was a military man who had served with Marius in Spain and again under his command in Africa, where he had distinguished himself in one of the critical battles against Jugurtha at Muthal. Rufus and Marius appear to have been on good terms, for all that Marius deliberately adopted a slightly uncouth image while Rufus was a highly cultured student of philosophy, a distinguished orator and, in his later years, a historian. Like Marius, Rufus was deeply interested in army reform and even today historians debate how much of Marius' later reorganization was based upon Rufus' recommendations, and also to what extent Marius simply took the credit for reforms which Rufus had already instituted while he was consul in this year.

The major factor in the election was the need to choose commanders for what everyone assumed would be a decisive clash that year with the Cimbri, who were now gathering on the frontier of Roman territory in Gaul. And, indeed, it appeared that the Roman assembly had picked the commanders carefully for the coming campaign.

Both consuls were new men, and since both were friends with Marius it was likely that they had compatible views and would work together in the field. Each man would command one consular army, but the senior consul would be Rufus, a man with considerable military experience and competence. As the choice of the people, the legionaries would follow both more enthusiastically than they would yet another aristocratic placeman, and trust to Rufus' experience to keep them safe.

None of this sat well with the aristocracy. From their perspective the campaign against the Cimbri was going to go badly no matter what. If the new consuls did as expected and crushed the enemy then the perceived wisdom of choosing non-aristocrats – a wisdom already demonstrated by the selection and subsequent victories of Marius in Africa – would be further confirmed with victory in Gaul. If, on the other hand, the new consuls followed the disastrous example of their aristocratic predecessors in campaigns against the Cimbri, then Rome would be defeated and that would not help anyone. The ideal solution would be for the Cimbri to be defeated, but with at least one of the aristocracy's own members on hand to claim the credit. Fortunately, the very man was right on the spot, Quintus Servilius Caepio, the other consul of 106 BC who was already on campaign in Gaul.

The Servilian family (the name Servilius means something like 'preserver', which is what the aristocracy hoped that this particular Servilius would do for their reputation) were extremely aristocratic. According to Livy, the family pre-dated the Republic and allegedly came from the ancient home of Rome's founders, the now-vanished city of Alba. True, the Caepiones were a relatively new branch of this aristocratic family tree, known only from the third century, and it has been suggested that the name was from a lost Etruscan root. (The alternative is a completely different root, namely *caepa*, or 'onion'.)

The Caepiones had produced two generals in the past few generations, both outstanding for the wrong reasons. There was the Caepio who was consul in 203 BC who proved so erratic that the Senate recalled him from the field, and the father of the Caepio now in Gaul. Caepio senior had campaigned in Spain, starting a war by violating an existing treaty and then, finding that he was not winning (mainly because his own soldiers hated him so much that the cavalry once tried to lynch him), he had finished the war by treachery. That is, he paid assassins to murder the enemy leader and when the men turned up for their reward Caepio had them killed instead.

Which brings us to the current Caepio, now proconsul of Transalpine Gaul. The main task of that consul was to protect the road which allowed Roman troops to march to the continual wars in Spain without the hazards of a sea journey. (During the Punic wars, disasters at sea had killed more Romans than Hannibal.) Caepio interpreted part of his brief as being to subdue the Gallic city of Tolosa – modern Toulouse – which had formerly been aligned with Rome but which had become restive after Rome's series of setbacks in the region. It is uncertain whether the city had openly allied with the Cimbri as some sources claim, but at the very least it was certainly sympathetic to the invading newcomers.

There has been considerable scepticism, both ancient and modern, as to whether Caepio's interest in Tolosa was due to that city's strategic position since it was over a hundred kilometres from the road Caepio was allegedly protecting. Certainly, Tolosa was not the only Gallic centre to repudiate Rome after the defeat of Cassius Longinus, so there was no real military or political reason for Caepio to single out Tolosa for the attention of the legions. But one need not look further for a reason than Tolosa's immense wealth.

Tolosa had long been a religious centre where gold and silver dedicated to the gods had accumulated to the point where some of it was literally tossed into lakes rather than packed into temple storehouses. Adding to this already vast stock of bullion, men from the Tectosages (the local Gallic tribe) had taken part in the raid on the Greek sanctuary of Delphi in which the Cimbri had also participated (see p.6) and had brought home with them a considerable amount of booty.

Caepio duly captured and sacked Tolosa, and sent a fortune in bullion back to Rome. This included 15,000 talents in gold ingots and treasure plus a lesser amount of silver. (By modern valuation this amounts to around £20,400,000,000, give or take a hundred million pounds or so.) Somehow the gold never reached Rome but mysteriously vanished along the route in what remains the largest theft ever carried out by non-government perpetrators.

If Caepio was responsible for the theft, as many believed, then he certainly had the money to bribe those senators responsible for allocating consular commands for the coming year. But as mentioned already, he would have been pushing at an open door because the aristocratic faction wanted one of their own people in command of at least one consular army anyway.

As last year's consul, Caepio in 105 BC was now a proconsul – a consular commander whose command had been prorogued, that is extended. This meant that if Caepio did get command of one of the consular armies destined for Gaul then he would be junior to whichever consul arrived with the other army. That the highly bred Caepio would be taking orders from a jumped-up nobody was a blatant contravention of the natural order of things, so Caepio had no intention of listening to instructions from whomever his consular colleague was going to be.

Of Rome's consuls for the year, Mallius Maximus would be a lot easier to ignore. By any standard P. Rutilius Rufus was a far better commander than either Caepio or Mallius, and everyone knew it. If ignoring Rutilius Rufus led to Rome's legions getting into difficulty, then Caepio would be held responsible. Even if Caepio was present when the Romans beat the Cimbri everyone would nevertheless assume that the enemy had been defeated by Rutilius Rufus, with Caepio in a subordinate role. If, on the other hand, the Cimbri were beaten under the command of Caepio's equal in incompetence, Mallius Maximus, then Caepio could certainly claim the lion's share of the credit. His claim would be even stronger if Caepio could demonstrate that he had not been paying much attention to Mallius in any case.

Thus we can assume that the fateful decision was taken through the machinations of back-room powerbrokers within the Roman Senate. Caepio would command one army in Gaul as proconsul, and Mallius Maximus would command the other. Rutilius Rufus, the man best placed to defeat the Cimbric horde, would remain in Rome for the duration of the campaign. (This is only an assumption, because we cannot discount more mundane but less likely scenarios, such as Rutilius Rufus being at the time too unwell or unwilling to undergo the rigours of a northern campaign.)

Howsoever it was arrived at, this was a decision that would cost the city tens of thousands of Roman lives and put the very existence of Rome under threat. It would also further enhance the reputation of the Roman aristocracy as lethally incompetent blunderers and thus fail to achieve even the cynical objectives for which Rutilius Rufus was probably excluded from command in the first place.

To help guide the inexperienced Mallius Maximus, the Senate appointed for him an aristocratic second-in-command, Marcus Aurelius Scaurus, who had served as consul three years previously. Not a great deal is known about the military abilities of Scaurus and he certainly did not demonstrate any in his first and only clash with the Cimbri.

As was usual with a senior legate, Scaurus' particular responsibility was the cavalry. It appears that on arrival in Gaul he took a large force of horsemen scouting north over the river Rhone in order to locate the Cimbri. The enemy were known to be present in large numbers, but their exact position was unknown. In one way at least, the mission was successful – either Scaurus found the Cimbri or the Cimbri found him.

Presumably some form of military action followed, with some modern historians asserting on dubious grounds that Scaurus' forward camp was overrun by the Cimbric horde. In fact, all that our sources tell us is that Scaurus 'lost his army' and was himself thrown from his horse while fighting.

What happened next is the sort of story that every national propaganda machine loves to propagate, and which should be distrusted for that very reason. Our main source is a sketchy historian of the second century AD called Granius Licinianus, (*History* 33), though for the late Republic he seems to have drawn his material from the more reliable (but now lost) works of Livy. According to Granius, not only did Scaurus survive his fall, but he was captured and hauled into the presence of the Cimbric leadership. Falling off a horse is credible enough but less probable is the idea that Scaurus was thereafter set on suicide 'out of shame that he should survive when so many of his men had been killed'. According to Granius, Scaurus deliberately infuriated the Cimbri with a severe lecture about the power of Rome and the inevitable fate that awaited the Cimbric horde should they dare to set foot in Italy. We reach the height of improbability with the claim that the Cimbri were so impressed by the Roman's resolution and fortitude that they offered him his life if he would consent to become their leader. 'Thus, though he could have escaped death', remarks Granius piously, 'he chose to do and say nothing unworthy of a Roman who had held such great honours'.

Scaurus was duly executed. The geographer Strabo tells us how that execution may have happened.

Their women participate in military excursions, and bring their priestesses with them. These wear ceremonial linen scarves and white robes fastened with a bronze belt and buckle. After a battle they go barefoot through the camp with unsheathed swords to examine the captives. Those whom they select are crowned with garlands and taken to a large platform which contains a bronze basin capable of holding 20 amphorae [around 1,000 litres].

The priestess mounts the stage and cuts the throat of each captive in succession, draining the blood into the basin. [Assuming each prisoner is fully drained, the basin could accommodate a maximum of around 200 victims.] From the blood collected in this manner they make prophecy which is confirmed by other priestesses who then disembowel the victims so that the entrails might tell of future victories. (Strabo *Geography*, 7)

From Strabo it is therefore possible to suggest an alternative version of Scaurus' warning, delivered not orally but by way of his entrails. If the Cimbric priestesses had (correctly) divined from the sacrifice of their noble victim that only doom awaited the tribe if they crossed into Italy, then the Cimbric leadership may have taken this warning from their gods much more seriously than a harangue from an aristocratic Roman. If so, then subsequent events show that Scaurus may well have saved Rome by his – literal – sacrifice.

Meanwhile, Mallius Maximus and Caepio had their expected falling-out. Mallius told Caepio what to do and Caepio carefully did the opposite. The soldiers, well aware that their necks were on the line if their commanders could not get their act together, relayed their concerns up through the chain of command. Caepio, well aware that mutinous troops had come close to killing his father, agreed to their demands. The two generals agreed to settle their differences at a conference but the meeting did not go well. As the historian Cassius Dio describes it:

> Caepio was forced by the soldiers to go and discuss the situation with Mallius. This did not lead to the two coming to an agreement but rather the opposite, for instead of finding a way of working together they ended up even more hostile than previously. The meeting collapsed into quarrel and insults and the pair parted in a disgraceful manner. (Dio, 29.31)

Thereafter, according to Orosius, the two armies acted independently, with the River Rhone acting as the *de facto* dividing line between their separate spheres of operation.

According to Granius Lucianus even the gods themselves tried to point out that things were on course for a disaster. In the Sabine country a statue of Mars the war god toppled onto its head, a deranged Roman lady sat herself on the throne of Jupiter in the Capitol, and when trumpet players blew to announce the Games, a swarm of black snakes suddenly appeared, bit and otherwise terrified bystanders, and then as suddenly vanished. (Granius Lucianus, 34)

Ignorant of these dire omens, the armies of Caepio and Mallius Maximus were engaged in a delicate dance between themselves and the advancing Cimbri. Mallius wanted the two Roman armies to join and fight the Cimbri as a combined unit, and Caepio was determined to maintain an independent command. However, recognizing that the climax of the campaign was approaching, Caepio did agree to cross the Rhone and put himself on the same side of the river as Mallius Maximus and the Cimbri. According to Dio, the two armies ended up encamped on either side of the larger Cimbric horde. This was hardly an ideal situation for co-ordinated action, even if either commander were capable of it.

The arrival of a second Roman army troubled the Cimbri, for even after their string of victories they had never underestimated the military prowess of the Roman army. Accordingly, they shifted their camp to be better positioned to withstand attack from one or the other army, or both combined. Then they sent envoys to see if they could resolve matters through negotiation. Probably because they had by now a considerable number of Roman prisoners, the Cimbri knew the correct protocol in these matters, and they accordingly sent their envoys to negotiate with the most senior Roman commander present, who happened to be Mallius Maximus.

This sent Caepio into what one historian described as a fit of 'mad jealousy'. So insulted was he by by his exclusion from negotiations that we are told that he would have personally slain the Cimbric ambassadors had he the chance. For Caepio there was now the terrifying possibility that Mallius Maximus might persuade the Cimbri to withdraw northwards, and the war would be ended peacefully – with all the credit going to an undeserving demagogic peasant rather than his aristocratic self.

No-one says that this was the reason why Caepio unilaterally decided that he was going to bypass the ongoing negotiations and lead his army to attack the Cimbric horde while its leaders were away talking to Mallius, but this is only because nobody says much about the Battle of Arausio at all. Roman historians seldom liked to dwell on Roman defeats, let alone defeats directly caused by the blundering of the Roman elite (whom the historians after all depended upon for financial support and patronage). Furthermore, there are no historians whose coherent accounts of this period have survived, apart from Sallust who was preoccupied with his Jugurthine War. Finally, though often called to account for his actions, Caepio never divulged what was going through what might loosely be described as his mind as he ordered his vastly outnumbered army into battle.

Therefore, what happened on that grim day (6 October, 105 BC – at least that much is known) alongside the river near Arausio must be mostly a matter of speculation. Mallius was still negotiating with the Cimbric leaders when word reached his camp that Caepio was attacking the enemy. What happened to the Cimbric negotiators thereafter is unknown – possibly they returned to their camp, for Granius Licinianus says that Caepio only attacked after the end of the first day of negotiations (in which the Cimbri again asked for land and were again brusquely refused).

Caepio's assault certainly had the desired effect in that peace talks with the Cimbri were immediately abandoned and both Roman armies attempted a military solution. The problem is that neither army knew what the other was doing and their commanders were working at crossed purposes. It is almost certain that Caepio's army engaged first, and if Plutarch's numbers are right for the Cimbri and Cassius Dio's numbers are correct for the Romans, then Caepio plunged his men into an engagement with the odds stacked at almost ten to one against him.

One can imagine a scenario where the army of Caepio ploughed into the Cimbric army, making slow progress against a stubborn enemy whose deep formation prevented the Romans from breaking through their battle line. Meanwhile, in Mallius Maximus' camp the legions who believed they had some time off while negotiations were underway had abruptly to march out to battle with no preparation whatsoever.

It did not help that the Romans were low on cavalry. This is probably one reason why Mallius had wanted Caepio nearby before the battle began. With the defeat of Aemilius Scaurus, Mallius had lost a good proportion of his cavalry and he needed help from Caepio's horsemen. When a force was as badly outnumbered as the Roman armies were, cavalry were essential to prevent the enemy infantry from rolling around the flanks and enveloping the army. As it was, even reinforced by Caepio's cavalry, the Romans would struggle. The Cimbri had plenty of cavalry and if they were up to the standard of Germanic cavalry they could probably have beaten the Roman horse even one to one. (Caesar later preferred German mercenary cavalrymen to Roman and asserted that they were immensely superior to the Gallic.)

Inevitably, Caepio's army was overwhelmed by sheer force of numbers and eventually pushed back against the Rhone. Or so we can assume from the fact that one of the very few survivors – a young officer called Quintus Sertorius – survived by swimming across. If the collapsing army of Caepio attempted to fall back upon their camp, the manoeuvre failed because the Cimbri swarmed right in after them and captured the place. Out of fear of the Romans, or perhaps to ensure that they never had to fight them again, the Cimbri did not bother with gesture warfare such as putting their enemies under the yoke. Disdaining attempts to surrender, they simply butchered every one of Caepio's men that they could get their hands upon.

Therefore, it is quite possible that by the time that Mallius' army took the field Caepio's army was either destroyed or well on the way to being so. Thus, instead of the Cimbri fighting a combined Roman army which they outnumbered five to one, they twice swarmed over an enemy whom they outnumbered ten to one. This places the responsibility for tens of thousands of Roman deaths directly at Caepio's door, for odds of five to one were actually fairly reasonable given Roman tactical superiority at the point of conflict. Certainly, Roman armies before and since had considerable success under such circumstances. But, if the odds were indeed ten to one, the Romans had the choice of being outflanked or of stretching their battle line impossibly thin. His army faced almost certain defeat whichever option Mallius Maximus took, and subsequently, as with Caepio, his army was overwhelmed and the legionaries massacred.

Less than a dozen men survived the debacle, making this a Roman disaster at least equal to the more famous defeat at Cannae at the hands of Hannibal a century before. The estimate of sixty thousand Roman casualties at Arausio is on the conservative side, for Granius Licinianus gives the figure of 80,000 men, claiming that this comes directly from the works of Rutilius Rufus. Orosius, following the lost text of an earlier historian, describes the disaster and aftermath in this manner:

In the six hundred and forty second year from the founding of the city C. Mallius and Q. Caepio, proconsul, went against the Cimbri, Teutones, Tigurini and Ambrones, tribes of Gaul and Germany. These were then closing on the Roman lands via the provinces through which flows the Rhone River. Here envy and discord caused the most damaging dispute between them, and brought great shame and danger to the name of Rome.

They were defeated … 80,000 Romans and their allies were slaughtered, along with 40,000 camp followers, according to [the historian] Antias. So complete was the destruction of all the army that only ten men survived.

Having gained possession of both camps and of a huge amount of booty, the enemy seemed as though driven by a strange and unusual curse. They completely destroyed everything they had captured, clothing was cut to pieces and strewn about, gold and silver were thrown into the river, the breastplates of the men were hacked to pieces, the trappings of the horses were ruined, the horses themselves were drowned in the water. Men had nooses fastened around their necks and were hanged from trees.

Thus the conqueror seized no booty, while the vanquished received no mercy. (Orosius, *History* 5.15 -16)

Chapter 6

Aftermath

S uch was the scale of the Roman defeat that there was no way of hiding the magnitude of the disaster from the Roman public. Too many families had lost husbands, sons and brothers, and these losses were not just among the common footsoldiers of Rome and the city's allies. Aristocratic families, both in Rome and among allies such as the Latins and the Marsi, had suffered also. After the battle, 'all Italy was filled with dread' remarks Sallust, yet, as the news filtered down through the Italian peninsula, with fear came anger. The Roman Senate came under increasing pressure to investigate the causes of the disaster and to hold accountable those responsible.

It certainly did not help that, although only a handful of men had escaped from the catastrophe that had destroyed two complete Roman armies, both commanders had made sure that they got out of it with their own skins intact. Mallius had lost both his sons in the battle, while Caepio had lost nothing, including his usual arrogance. Now powerful forces were lining up against the incompetent proconsul.

For a start, one of the few remaining checks on the power of the Roman aristocracy was the ambition of younger members of that same aristocracy. It was generally agreed that one way for an aspiring politician to jump-start his career was by successfully prosecuting a more senior senator for crimes real or imagined. The bigger the name and reputation of the man so prosecuted, the greater the status earned by the prosecutor who took him down, not least because senior Romans took getting prosecuted very personally and a failed prosecution could mark the end of a promising career.

However, Caepio's leading role in the disaster at Arausio had left him vulnerable, for suddenly Caepio, the well-connected and powerful back-room operator, had no friends to guard his back. Roman aristocrats were, above all, politicians and the name of Caepio had become so toxic with the public that no-one with a reputation to lose wanted anything to do with him. The question became not whether Caepio would be prosecuted but who would succeed in grabbing the prize of leading that prosecution.

Furthermore, the supporters of Marius were very keen to unload the lion's share of the blame for Rome's catastrophic defeat upon Caepio's richly-deserving shoulders and thus avoid the suggestion that the loss of Rome's armies was due to the election of a non-aristocrat to the consulship.

Mallius himself was considered disposable and Marius – who knew a thing or two about political expediency – did nothing to defend his man when the firebrand tribune Saturninus had Mallius prosecuted and exiled for his role in the disaster. Instead, Marius and his supporters concentrated on ensuring that whatever punishment Mallius suffered, Caepio would get the same, only hotter and stronger.

This was duly arranged in a series of slow, vindictive steps. First the people passed a law that stripped Caepio of his rank as proconsul. Then a tribune proposed and passed a law that any person stripped of his rank by the people should also be expelled from the Senate.

At this point an attempt was made to charge Caepio with expropriating the vanished gold which he had looted from Tolosa. Caepio escaped this charge mainly because two aspiring tribunes prevented that case from going forward. This was not out of love for Caepio, but because the tribunes wanted him intact so that they could demolish him personally. They went on to duly charge Caepio with the 'negligent loss of his army' and encouraged the jury to think of the most severe punishment that they could contrive. Probably to the great regret of the jurors, the death penalty was not an option because Roman law was remarkably lenient in this regard, and the courts seldom allowed Romans to execute their own citizens. Instead, the jury fined Caepio 15,000 talents of gold – a sum so massive that one must assume that the idea was that if ever such a sum (e.g. the booty of Tolosa) turned up in Caepio's possession, the Roman people could take it without argument. Lacking immediate access to the treasure, the Roman people made do for now by annexing all of Caepio's property and assets – a move unprecedented in the Republic.

Next, Caepio was stripped of Roman citizenship. By one dubious account, since Caepio then was no longer a citizen and could therefore be legitimately executed, the Romans proceeded to do just that. More credible accounts tell us that Caepio was driven into exile once the jury decided he was subject to a law declaring that no-one within 800 miles of Rome was permitted to give him even the basics of life (literally fire or water). Caepio duly went to live in the city of Smyrna on the coast of Asia Minor, where he remained disgraced and forgotten until his death. According to Strabo, the confiscation of all his assets left his female relatives in Rome so destitute that for a while they had to turn to prostitution to make ends meet.

That Rome had the time to set about punishing its incompetent generals through a leisurely process of law was because they had received intelligence that the Cimbric emergency, while still an existential threat to Rome, was apparently not as pressing as the Romans had initially thought. While the Romans regarded espionage as necessary, it was not a part of warfare with which any gentleman wished to be associated, and as a result Roman writers tell us little about how the Romans garnered the military intelligence which Rutilius Rufus was now using to track the enemy's movements.

It is reported that the Romans had recruited Gauls who joined the Cimbri and these men passed back reports of the enemy army's whereabouts and intentions. Also, after Arausio, Rome's surviving consul had the further benefit of reports from a more senior source. This was that enterprising young aristocrat called Quintus Sertorius who had saved himself from the general massacre of the Roman army by swimming across the river – no mean feat since he was fully clad in armour at the time. As one of the handful of men who had survived a battle which had killed tens of thousands, Sertorius evidently felt he had not pushed his luck far enough. Therefore, he joined the Cimbric horde as a spy. Plutarch reports:

> He dressed as a Celt and learned enough of the basics of the language to carry out a rudimentary conversation if he had to. Thereafter he blended in with the barbarians and once he had gathered intelligence of sufficient importance, he returned. (Plutarch, *Sertorius* 3)

The idea that an Italian aristocrat could pass as a Celt by putting on trousers is as laughable as the idea that a modern Egyptian could pass as a Scotsman by donning a kilt. Rather than follow Plutarch and assume that because they were barbarians the Cimbri were stupid, we should accept that the Cimbri were well aware of the identity of the Italian in their ranks.

Just as the Romans did, the Cimbri would have gathered military intelligence for themselves using prisoners and their own Gallic spies. They would have known that at this time Rome's Italian allies were as disillusioned with the arrogance, corruption and incompetence of the Senate as were the Roman commoners themselves. (In fact, a decade after the Cimbric wars, the patience of the allies ran out and they rebelled against Rome.) That an Italian aristocrat – Sertorius was from a well-off Oscan family – might choose to throw in his lot with the Cimbri was not all that surprising, and the newcomer may well have been welcomed in the hope that other disaffected Italians would be encouraged to join him.

The question now facing the Cimbri was what to do next. Certainly, they had defeated the Romans, but as they had defeated the Romans in Gaul they were no nearer to finding a homeland for themselves, and they were rapidly wearing out their welcome with the Gallic tribes. One logical course would be for the Cimbri to do as the Romans were dreading and follow up their victory, cross the Alps and settle in Italy. Yet this again assumes that the Cimbri had not done their homework. It is highly probable that the Cimbri were well aware that Hannibal had crossed into Italy a century before. It is true that Hannibal had crushed a Roman army (or three) in Italy while the Cimbri had done it in Gaul, but after great initial success, Hannibal had gradually been ground down by Rome's superior manpower and the advantages of the Italian terrain, which was well suited for defensive warfare.

It was now close to autumn. Should the Cimbri cross the Alps, they ran the risk of the passes closing behind them as winter set in, leaving them stranded in Italy with no option but to conquer or die. Even after a series of victories over the Romans the Cimbri did not underestimate their enemies, and they would have known – that homework again – that the Romans were never more dangerous than when they had their backs to the wall. Also, Rome was far from defenceless. His absence from the disaster at Arausio had at least left the highly competent consul Rutilius Rufus in charge of the aftermath in Rome. Rutilius had first made those young men eligible for the levy swear an oath that they would not leave Italy, and thereafter he started to recruit them into a small but highly-competent army.

One innovation that Rutilius Rufus used was to take gladiators and their trainers from the arena and use them to teach his own drill sergeants how to instruct the new legionaries in combat techniques, fitness and diet. Meanwhile, the consul kept a close eye on the Cimbri and was ready to march north and defend the Alpine passes if need be.

Rufus need only hold back the Cimbri until reinforcements arrived – these reinforcements being the veteran army of Marius which was now headed for home after the capture of Jugurtha and the end of the Numidian war. Incompetent generalship had delivered the Romans to the Cimbri at Arausio, but the Cimbri correctly reckoned that Marius and Rutilius Rufus were quite a different proposition.

Therefore, rather than take an all-or-nothing gamble, the Cimbric leadership decided to move on and see whether they could find somewhere to settle over the Pyrenees in Iberia. By Cimbric reasoning, Italy was not going anywhere and, if they failed in Spain, Italy still remained as a last resort. Accordingly, as hordes of Germans would do millennia later, the Cimbri decided to head to Spain for the winter.

This was reasonable enough, though in retrospect there was one glaring flaw in the Cimbric plan. The Cimbri assumed that the Romans and their army were now a known quality – and that their own qualities were superior. In this assumption the Cimbric leadership underestimated Roman pragmatism or the extent to which Roman defeats had delivered a kick in the pants to those complacent forces in the Senate which had resisted reform. It had now become apparent that, when it came to fighting the Cimbri, the Roman army was not fit for purpose – something which many had come to suspect after the uphill work Rome had made of the Numidian campaign – and a drastic overhaul was needed.

The Roman people signalled their willingness for change with the elections for the consuls of 104 BC. The competent Quintus

Lutatius Catulus had offered himself as a candidate, but the voters were in no mood to have another member of an old Roman family in the top job, however well qualified he may be. Instead, for the second year running they ignored the established aristocracy and elected a *novus homo*, a man called Flavius Fimbria. Fimbria was a competent jurist and an orator of some skill, but his main qualification was that he was prepared to obediently subordinate himself to the other consul of the year. This consul was the same as the previous year's consul, Gaius Marius.

Technically speaking, Marius should not have been elected, for the Roman constitution did not allow a man to stand for the consulship *in absentia*, and at the time of his election Marius was still in Africa wrapping up the last details of the Numidian war. Furthermore, a consul was expected to step aside after his year in office and allow a decent interval to pass before the extremely rare event that he offered himself once more for election. For a man to stand for consul twice in three years was a rude violation of convention, although not a technical breach of the Roman constitution.

All this the Roman voters ignored with a fine disdain, believing that getting the right man to deal with the Cimbric threat overrode any concern for conventional niceties. Plutarch sums up how the Roman people considered their enemies at that time. He says that the people felt that

> The Cimbri possessed irresistible bravery and audacity, sweeping down on the enemy in battle like a powerful wall of fire which no-one could stand against. The Cimbri saw not enemies but victims and loot, even if they were looking at large Roman armies. Those [Roman] generals charged with protecting Transalpine Gaul had not only failed ingloriously, but their pathetic resistance had only encouraged the onrushing Cimbri to consider descending

upon Italy itself. The barbarians had now determined not to settle anywhere before they had destroyed Rome and pillaged Italy. (Plutarch, *Marius* 11)

It was a nightmarish prospect, and in the eyes of the voters only Marius stood between that ghastly vision and it becoming reality. For once the Roman Senate decided to accept what it could not change. The people of Rome wanted Marius – well then, let them have him. Even the most reactionary members of the oligarchy recognized that, if the truth be told, the voters could have chosen far worse a man to lead Rome through the dark days ahead.

Accordingly Marius returned to Rome and on his arrival promptly boosted public morale by celebrating a splendid triumph for his African war. Exhibit A in the triumphal parade was Jugurtha himself, captured and paraded through the city he had so recently disdained. After the triumphal parade, Marius sat down to a state banquet knowing that at the same time in the dungeons below Jugurtha was being ritually strangled. Then, with the distraction of the war in Africa finally in the past, Marius and his subordinates turned their full attention to the issue of what to do about the Cimbri if and when they returned to threaten Italy once more.

Interestingly, even though he now had with him in Italy the army which he had led to victory in Africa, Marius chose to step aside from direct command of these men and instead put himself at the head of the smaller but arguably better-trained army raised by his former colleague Rutilius Rufus. It was also at this point that Marius set about reshaping the Roman army into the instrument of conquest which would go on to dominate the Mediterranean world in the coming century.

The first of these reforms was already in place – no longer were Roman soldiers men of a certain property class who brought their own equipment to war with them. The lack of men needed for the African war had forced Marius to recruit from and equip the *caput censi* – that class of voter who, if they fought at all in previous wars, were limited to fighting as skirmishers on the outskirts of the main battle. As a result of the integration of these men into the legions Rome now had a class of soldier who was committed to the military as a career.

Heretofore the average legionary had a farm or business to which he wanted to return once he had completed the campaign for which he had been called up. Recruiting men who had nowhere to go once they were stood down after their campaigns was a dangerous step that was certain to lead to considerable political instability. However, even if the issue was foreseeable, Marius could justifiably claim that his measures, while they may have been storing up problems for Rome in the future, were justified in the present in order to ensure that Rome actually had a future.

Furthermore, once Rome had trained and equipped a soldier who had nowhere to go once his campaign was over, the next logical step was to keep that soldier under arms for as long as possible. Even if there was no war currently under way, Rome's enterprising politican-generals were quite capable of finding or provoking one. Indeed, one factor driving the massive expansion of Roman territory in the last years of the Republic was because Rome now had an army of trained professionals ready to get aggressive at a moment's notice. If these men were not fighting a foreign enemy they needed to be stood down and would immediately thereafter become a menace to domestic peace.

Since the *caput censi* could barely support themselves, they could certainly not buy their own equipment and bring that to war. Based upon what a modern military re-enactor would pay to purchase a full set of replica late Republican army equipment, it seems reasonable to assume that – given the greater difficulty in antiquity of manufacturing things like the metal loops for chain mail – a full set of armour and weaponry would easily have cost a poor Roman more than a year's income. Therefore, the cost of equipping a legion fell upon the state or, more particularly, became the responsibility of whatever consul was raising the army.

Because Roman military gear was now manufactured in industrial quantities, this equipment became standardized to an unprecedented degree. Swords had been something of a random selection depending on what family heirlooms or local manufactories could come up with. Now all soldiers were equipped with the *gladius hispaniensis*, the Roman short stabbing sword which was to terrify enemies for the next five hundred years. Following the regime established by Rutilius Rufus and his gladiator trainers, legionaries practised for hours at a time hacking and stabbing at a wooden post with a *rudus* – a wooden sword designed to be slightly heavier than the real thing. If the legionaries were stuck at the front of the battle line for an extended period, their enemies' sword arms would probably tire first.

The heavy throwing spear, the *pilum*, was standardized and consequently the range of these weapons fell into a standard distance also. Legionaries trained in throwing their spears as a co-ordinated unit, while shields of a standard size made drill and intra-unit manoeuvres simpler to execute. Thus, with standard equipment, better training and greater experience, Roman legionaries were able to fight in even-tighter formations. This meant that local superiority in combat was even greater and even more legionaries would be facing the same number of barbarian opponents at the point where the battle lines met.

The Marian reforms also recognized that while maniples of legionaries were excellent for chasing Iberian tribal irregulars around the broken terrain of Spain (one of the main occupations of Roman soldiery after the Punic wars), the legions needed greater solidity if they were to withstand the fury of a head-on Cimbric charge. Therefore the maniple was discarded, and

Roman military formations were bulked up by the creation of the cohort as the main tactical unit of the army.

If the cohort was the main tactical unit, the fundamental unit of the Roman army became the *contubernium*. This was a squad of eight men about which the rest of the army was built, rather as houses are built of basic bricks. *Contubernium* literally means 'tenting together', which is what the men of the *contubernium* did. These men kept their supplies together and bunked in a single tent while on campaign. They also shared a single pack mule for cooking and other equipment, and generally had one or two servants assigned to the group. Members of a *contubernium* were expected to look out for each other during the various complexities which develop when a large body of men are forced together in a stressful environment for a sustained period. To reinforce this solidarity, the men of a *contubernium* were usually rewarded or punished together as a group. Ten of these groups of eight made up a century, which was placed under a single officer, logically enough called a centurion.

The new tactical combat unit of the cohort was made up of six centuries, or a theoretical 480 legionaries. (The practical number varied depending on how many men were absent on detached duty, sick or wounded.) There was a complicated ranking system for centurions which was reflected in their positions in the cohort formation, but generally the most senior of these men was automatically the cohort commander. If the commander fell in action – not an unexpected event, because centurions were expected to lead by example – then the next-senior centurion took over, and so on until the cohort ran out of either centurions or legionaries.

The plum job for a legionary centurion was to command the first cohort of the legion. This cohort was twice the size of the other cohorts and was manned by the most-experienced soldiers. The centurion in command was called the 'first spear' or *primus pilius*.

This man and the prefect of the camp – the man in charge of the legion's day-to-day logistics – were expected to work closely with the legion or army commander, who at this time was generally a consul, proconsul or praetor. On the other end of the scale was the tenth cohort, the bucket into which were poured the legion's green troops, riff-raff and hopeless cases. One might assume that depending upon the circumstances and what the commander was expecting to achieve, the first or tenth cohorts were most often in the thick of the action.

Each legion of ten cohorts was supported by a small cavalry contingent of around 120 men, and these plus officers brought the theoretical strength of a legion up to 5,000 men. In practice most legions were somewhat smaller.

Marius had learned much during the earlier wars in which he had fought against Spanish guerrillas and the highly mobile Numidians (who were generally reckoned to have the finest light cavalry in the known world). One of the things he had learned was that a lightly armed enemy could run rings around the ponderous Roman army. While it was impossible to make the army as mobile as many of Rome's enemies, Marius could at least speed it up somewhat. One way he did so was simply by making his men faster – 'he carefully disciplined and trained his army whilst they were on the move, making them practise route marches, and running of every kind,' remarks Plutarch.

Next, Marius slimmed down the ponderous baggage train which both encumbered an army and was one of its most vulnerable points. He did this by making each soldier carry more of his own equipment along with several days of rations. Thereafter a Roman legionary on the march had the dubious privilege of carrying around fifty pounds of gear, including entrenching equipment and armour. Much of this was placed on a long pole called a *furca*, which was carried over the shoulder.

From this load came the slang expression for a legionary, 'Marius' mule', though Plutarch gives an alternative explanation also. This is that when Scipio Aemilianus was campaigning in Spain he was mightily impressed by a mule which Marius used to carry his gear, and frequently commented on the superb condition of the animal. Thereafter the legionaries used the term 'Marius' mule' for the type of dogged trooper, beloved of his superiors, who conscientiously laboured through all his duties without complaint.

It was also Marius who made the eagle the standard standard for every legion, replacing other emblems which had included the ox, the boar and the minotaur. The legion's eagle now became a revered symbol of that legion, carried by a special standard-bearer called the *aquilifer* who received double pay, partly as recompense for becoming a javelin magnet in combat. The soldiers were indoctrinated with the idea that the eagle embodied the spirit of the legion and that the loss of an eagle was the worst disgrace that could befall the unit. This concept extended all the way up the ranks, and even in the Imperial era the Roman state made extraordinary efforts to regain eagles lost after a defeat. The other legionary symbols remained but were now very much secondary.

These reforms did not happen overnight but were the product of slow experimentation as Marius drilled and reshuffled his troops, keeping them in a state of constant readiness for the return of the Cimbri. In fact, at this point the Cimbri had split from their allies the Ambrones, Teutones and Tigurini. The Cimbri were eager to see if they could carve out a new homeland for themselves in Iberia, while the allied tribes had homelands already. Since the horde had by now fallen out with the Gauls who had been their reluctant hosts, the allied tribes reckoned they may as well stay and plunder the place, which they proceeded to do.

There is little information on how the Cimbri fared in Iberia, but it is safe to assume that theirs was not a pleasant sojourn. The local tribes may have lacked the cohesion and discipline of the Roman legions, but the previous century had given them a lot of practice at fighting those same legions, and by contrast the Cimbri must have come as light relief. The tough Cimbric heavy cavalry was less useful in broken Spanish terrain than it had been on the plains of Gaul, and the light Spanish irregular cavalry harassed them at every turn. The Cimbric infantry may have been introduced to the local speciality of the Cantabrian circle, where light cavalry formed a circle in front of an enemy infantry unit. As they galloped past the front of the enemy, the horsemen would let fly with javelins before wheeling away and re-arming at the part of the circle furthest from their targets. This meant that the part of the enemy line selected for punishment received a non-stop stream of missiles until it buckled.

Among the most formidable warriors of the peninsula were the Celtiberians, a people of allegedly Gallic descent who had made themselves at home in the heart of Spain. These men fought in close formation as heavy infantry, but with the support of swarms of light auxiliaries. However, the Celtiberians had been roughly handled by the Romans in the same campaign in which both Marius and Jugurtha had participated, and they were no longer the force which they once had been.

Those Celtiberians who survived did so in hilltop fortresses which the Romans – who were very skilled at siege warfare – had reckoned too tough to be worth the trouble. The Cimbri were not at all skilled in siege warfare and were at a loss as to how to storm the defences. As the Romans had discovered to their disgust in previous campaigns, even if one did make the effort to overwhelm a fortress over the objections of its fanatical defenders, the result was seldom worth it. Most Spanish forts held little of value, and in terms of conquest, once the bloody and exhausting business of taking a fort had been accomplished, there was always the next fort on the next hilltop.

Another problematic factor for the invaders was that the climate was more than somewhat different to that near the edge of the Arctic circle where the Cimbri had once dwelt. It is uncertain to what extent the brutal heat of a Spanish summer discombobulated the Cimbric army, but temperatures in the hottest part of the year often exceed 40 degrees Celsius (104 Fahrenheit) in modern Spain while those in Jutland seldom soar beyond half that figure. Acclimatization is more than a matter of the human body adjusting to the heat – certain social and cultural adjustments are sometimes harder to make, such as when to eat and sleep – or fight. (For example, even today many Danish restaurants close between nine and ten in the evening – at precisely the time that Spanish restaurants are just opening up for their customers.)

Finally, there was the issue of logistics. Much of Iberia was far from ideal farming country, and this presented huge difficulties when it came to supporting a mass of tens of thousands of men, women and children on the move. In the equally mountainous peninsula of Greece few armies of more than ten thousand men campaigned at a time, not because their generals did not want more men, but because it was too difficult to feed them. The situation was probably the same in Spain, and those fertile regions which could support a large population already did so and had little to share with new arrivals.

We know basically nothing about the travels of the Cimbric forces in Spain but we can assume that the Cimbri had perforce to try to occupy such areas as could feed a nation on the move, and also assume that the current owners of such areas vigorously held on to their produce. Since warfare is highly deleterious to agriculture, a season or two of fighting would force the Cimbric horde to move on to undevastated territory, there to repeat the cycle.

As an added complication, the Cimbri were not just fighting the natives. So deep were Rome's reserves of manpower that the Romans were able to simultaneously rebuild their armies after Arausio, fight an ongoing action with pirates in the eastern Mediterranean, attempt to contain the conflagration of the slave war in Sicily and still fight a vicious three-way war in Spain with the locals and the Cimbri. There is a confused reference by the fifth-century Obsequens which suggests that the Romans lost another army at this point, possibly to the Lusitanians, and the somewhat more contemporary Appian suggests that, deprived of reinforcements from Rome, a local commander allied with some Celtiberian tribes to help fight off the Cimbri.

One thing that can be safely stated about the Cimbric invasion of Spain is that the Cimbri did not easily give up their dream of an Iberian homeland. They tried for almost three years and only thereafter gave up and returned to Gaul. Meanwhile, the Teutones had plundered almost all that they could plunder from Gaul and were seeking new opportunities, while their allies the Tigurini had mostly packed up and returned to the Norican Alps. By and large the Ambrones stayed with the Teutones, but later reports imply that a good number of them also settled – then or later – among the Belgic tribes in northwest Gaul, a region where the natives later gave Julius Caesar considerable trouble.

From the viewpoint of the Teutones and those Ambrones who remained with them, Gaul was exhausted as a source of plunder. For the Cimbri, Iberia had proven an unsatisfactory choice of homeland. Both groups now turned their attention to the Italian peninsula and the rich, fertile plains north of Milan and in the Po valley.

After a respite of three years, the Cimbri were again marching on Rome. The issue now to be decided was whether the Romans had done enough to prepare to meet them.

Chapter 7

Into Italy

The Cimbric advance on Italy was no spontaneous, headlong charge. The Cimbric leaders were still wary of Rome's military prowess, and their previous string of victories had in no way caused them to underestimate the scale of the challenge that awaited them once they had decided to invade Italy. Therefore, the months before the actual Cimbric advance were spent in serious diplomacy and cautious, detailed planning.

Several centuries after the Cimbric wars, barbarian tribes which planned an attack over the Roman frontier carefully co-ordinated their efforts, knowing that the Roman army could usually only deal with one threat at a time. Therefore, an attack on multiple fronts by a combination of tribes stood a greater chance of success. It seems that the Cimbri were innovators in this regard, having developed this strategy in the late second century BC.

Their basic plan was to attack on two fronts after creating an alliance which would combine tribes with two different objectives. Some peoples like the Ambrones and Tigurini would consider the invasion of Italy as a huge raid with slaves and booty as the objective. The Cimbri, and possibly some of the Teutones, would take advantage of the chaos to achieve their purpose and move in on a permanent basis. There was a precedent for such a move.

We have seen that around a century and a half previously, a federation of tribes from Gaul and from across the Danube had joined forces in a massive raid on Greece. The raid was turned back by the combined efforts of the Greek city-states, but only after the raiders had inflicted considerable devastation. Yet, thereafter, one branch of the Gallic invasion force did not return home but continued moving east. This group eventually arrived in Asia Minor and by exploiting the political divisions between and within the different kingdoms in the area they eventually managed to claw out a homeland for themselves in the heartlands of Anatolia.

Now known as the Galatians, the people of this outpost of Gallic culture in Asia Minor survived for centuries as a distinct people and culture. They were eventually absorbed by the Roman empire and are best known today through a letter written by an itinerant evangelist; St Paul's Epistle to the Galatians is now a part of the Bible.

The Cimbri had spent considerable time in the original homeland of the Galatians, which was in southern Gaul. It follows that they would certainly have been aware of the Galatian success in establishing themselves comfortably in a new home on the other side of the Mediterranean, and they were keen to emulate this achievement in Italy. With this in mind, they informed all tribes north of the Alps that they intended to invade Italy and offered an open invitation to any individuals and groups who would like to join them in this opportunity of a lifetime for pillage and plunder.

Naturally the Teutones and Tigurini signed up, the former because their fate was by now inextricably linked to that of the Cimbri. The Tigurini joined in because they had already chopped up a Roman army under the unfortunate Cassius Longinus in 107 BC and knew full well that the Romans had very long memories for that sort of thing. If Rome survived the Cimbric assault it was only a matter of time before some enterprising consul decided to avenge Rome's defeat at their hands and promote his public image by bloodily conquering the tribe. The attack and crippling of Rome could therefore be considered almost an act of self-defence in their case.

The Cimbric recruiting drive also attracted some Helveti tribes, and also some 30,000 Ambrones were tempted from their new homeland in northwest Gaul to rejoin the invading horde. There were also individual volunteers from parts of Gaul where years of warfare had destroyed any means of survival other than a mercenary career. While the invaders accepted such men into their ranks, they did not trust them much – understandably, as it seems from hints in our sources that these volunteers included a number of Roman spies. Thereafter the Romans were well-informed about the movements and intentions of their attackers.

The result of this massive recruiting drive by the Cimbri was that the Romans had to face an even larger force than heretofore. When discussing this issue today, there is the usual vexed question of how much credibility to give the numbers listed by Roman historians. Here we shall simply present those numbers and ask the reader to accept that the true number was anywhere between full face value and ten per cent of the given figure. By Roman accounts the invasion force came to a massive horde of nearly half a million men, or three times the size of the allied invasion force on D-Day two thousand years later.

There was simply no way to supply so many men as a single army, and that was not the intention in any case. The Cimbri wanted to attack the Romans on two fronts in order to force their enemy to split their already-outnumbered army in half. Since each Roman army would be outnumbered ten to one, the invaders should be able to roll over them separately. This was especially true if one army should defeat the Romans first, after which the combined horde could descend upon Rome's last army with overwhelming force. In the unlikely event that one Roman army managed to hold back or even repel the attackers and join up with the other army, the combined Roman armies would still be outnumbered five to one by the other barbarian army.

Accordingly, the invasion force split up. One prong of the attack would strike Italy from the west, following the coast of Gaul with the intention of crossing the Piedmontese Alps in the footsteps of Hannibal. This force would be led by the Teutonic king, Teutobod, at the head of some 150,000 of his fellow tribesmen, and supported by around 25,000 Ambrones and other minor allies. According to Livy (*Epitome*, 68) the above count considerably underestimates the size of Teutobod's army, which he put at around 300,000 men.

The second prong of the attack would come from the east where Boiorix, king of the Cimbri, would return to Noricum, picking up whatever allies he could along the way. From there he would enter Italy through the Brenner Pass of the Alps and drive across the region today called Lombardy towards Milan. If we are to accept Plutarch's estimate of an original force of 300,000 Cimbri then this tribe alone made up a huge force. There may perhaps have been some attrition of the Cimbric force during their Iberian adventure, but any loss in numbers was compensated by the addition of the accompanying Tigurini, who, as mentioned, had already defeated a Roman army without assistance. The Tigurini would loop even further east and enter Italy via the Julian Alps, with their target being the fortress city of Aquelia, a city specifically founded in order to cope with transalpine attacks from that direction.

The Roman consul who was charged with throwing back this massive invasion was the same man who had been consul the previous year, and also for the year before the year before that, namely Caius Marius, now in an unprecedented fourth consulship.

As far as is known, the Romans did not have a written constitution, but instead they strictly followed a code called the *mos maiorum* – the ancestral tradition. Marius had already set one damaging precedent when he allowed the recruitment of the *caput censi* into the legions. Now he had set another precedent (later gratefully seized upon by Rome's first emperors) of holding multiple consecutive consulships.

In his first year, Marius had done what he did best; he had taken the new and slightly wary army created by Rutilius Rufus and moulded it into a force which trusted him completely. For a start, Marius showed that he was not a commander to be trifled with. He cowed the troops with occasional bursts of temper and with the severity of his punishments. Yet, at the same time, he was absolutely impartial and showed neither vindictiveness nor favouritism.

Marius was given the perfect opportunity to demonstrate this when his nephew was killed. This man had joined the army under his uncle's command, because the Romans regarded nepotism as a perfectly satisfactory method of filling such positions. The nephew developed an unfortunate fixation upon one of the soldiers in his unit and tried unsuccessfully to seduce the man, who was definitely not interested. Undeterred, the nephew summoned his would-be paramour to his tent one night, a summons which the soldier was unable to disobey since the command came from a superior officer.

An attempted seduction turned into an attempted rape, which ended with the planned victim drawing a sword and killing his attacker. The army expected that Marius would punish brutally the killer of his young relative. Instead, once Marius had heard the history of harassment that the young man had suffered, not only did he acquit him but he also gave him an award for meritorious conduct. Added to this exemplary example of non-favouritism, Marius continued his habit of eating the same meals as his troops and sharing their labours and hardships. By these practices, Plutarch tells us, he acquired a body of men both disciplined and loyal.

The army of Marius was an estimated 35,000 strong, and besides Rutilius Rufus' recruits it contained many of the veterans from his African campaign. After the reform which allowed *caput censi* to enrol in the legions, many of these were men with nowhere to go after their year in service. Many of these men happily re-enlisted year after year, giving Marius that rarest of creatures in the ancient world – a properly professional army. This army Marius took to the southeast of Gaul, for he had determined that, with the shorter route into Italy, the Teutones and their allies constituted the more immediate threat.

While waiting for the Teutones to arrive and test the mettle of his new fighting force, Marius kept the men busy with drills designed to accustom the men to the new formations in which they would be fighting. Since this was insufficient to occupy the troops full time, Marius also set the men to that other task for which the legions were to become famous – the creation of large-scale public works.

With the Rhone handily nearby, Marius set about dredging silt from the river to create a more navigable waterway, which would give him the means to rapidly move large numbers of troops upriver from Massalia without tiring them out. Marius bypassed entirely the boggy estuary near Massalia, digging the arrow-straight canal that was called the *fossa Mariana* for centuries thereafter. This canal, when later handed over to Massalia and used for commercial shipping, boosted the economic development of the entire region. The canal thereafter did much to engender goodwill toward Rome in a region where, at the time, such goodwill was in perilously short supply.

Marius' consulships had rolled from one to the next through the pragmatism which the Romans allowed to over-rule even their treasured traditions. At the end of Marius' first year of command he was in the middle of a major army re-organization. To turn over command at this delicate moment was a recipe for chaos which would be fatal should the Cimbri choose that moment to return to threaten Rome. Once the precedent was established, it seemed reasonable for Marius to be selected yet again, especially as a convenient rumour swept through Rome just before the elections that the Cimbri had indeed begun their long-feared march on the city. The rumour proved false and the Cimbri did not come, but this was only established once Marius had been safely re-elected.

By the time the next consular elections were due, even some pro-Marian Romans reckoned that enough was enough. Indeed, even Marius himself protested that he had held the consulship for long enough and it was time for him to step aside. At this, Saturninus, that demagogic tribune, stepped forward and castigated Marius as a traitor who would abandon Rome at the moment when his country needed him the most. Saturninus gave the voters an impassioned harangue in which he argued that the people should re-elect Marius whether he wanted to be consul or not. As Plutarch drily remarked:

> It was clear to everyone that Saturninus had been put up to this by Marius, and was playing a part – and playing it badly – but the people reckoned that they needed a man with the luck and ability of Marius and voted for him anyway. (Plutarch, Marius 14)

As Marius' colleague in what was to be a crucial year for the city, the voters chose Lutatius Catulus, a member of the old nobility, albeit of a family which had not won a consulship for over a century. Catulus was respected by his peers and was, if not well-regarded, at least not disliked by the common people, something that could not be said for many of the Roman nobility. Since one consul could veto the actions of another, it is very possible that there was a general feeling that someone with the political clout of a Catulus was needed. Should Marius let his string of consulships go to his head and become too dictatorial, Catulus had the connections and personal self-confidence to block his politically powerful colleague. Catulus was very wealthy and an accomplished poet, but of his military ability little is known before his consular year, a consular year that was long in coming. Catulus had stood and had been rejected by the electorate several times before he was elected as the junior consul for 101 BC.

While Catulus was not of a family with a great military background, Roman voters were great believers in eugenics and many might have been swayed by the career of the last consular ancestor of Catulus, this being Caius Lutatius Catulus, consul of 242 BC. This Catulus was partly responsible for bringing the First Punic War to a close when he defeated a large Carthaginian fleet – and that even though he had been incapacitated by a severe wound received in a previous engagement. This constituted the sort of inherited attribute that Roman voters felt they needed in a commander for the current desperate situation.

As the junior consul, Catulus was allocated command of the army facing what was considered to be the secondary threat – the attack of the Cimbri from the east. It is not that the Cimbri were considered any less dangerous than the Teutones and Ambrones, but because the Cimbri had to make their way around the Northern Alps to Noricum before advancing on Italy, while the Teutones and Ambrones were already on the doorstep.

It was also natural enough that Marius should take with him the army he had carefully trained and prepared for this moment. This left Catulus with the more-recent levy of troops – men less trained and prepared and whose morale suffered from the knowledge that the Roman army had not yet been able to beat the Cimbri in almost a decade of trying. On the other hand, rather than engage immediately in battle, Catulus had only to hurry to northeast Italy and try to hold the alpine passes.

Meanwhile, Marius would take a more proactive approach to the enemy and try to engage them early in battle. If all went according to plan, Marius might be able to defeat the Teutones and reinforce his colleague before he ever had to fight. This plan relied upon Marius aggressively engaging the enemy and Boiorix of the Cimbri taking a relatively leisurely stroll around the northern Alps. This went against the nature of both commanders, for Marius was a cautious general who only fought when he had to and when the odds or terrain were greatly in his favour, while Boiorix was more the type of commander inclined to seize events by the forelock and hurry them along. With Roman caution on the one hand and Cimbric celerity on the other, the chances were high that Catulus would be fighting the Cimbri on his own at least to start with – and so things transpired.

The invaders had going for them massive numbers and high morale based upon the fact that they had never yet been defeated by the Romans – although recent setbacks in Iberia might have somewhat blunted their high spirits, rather as their failure to do well against the Belgae might have rather subdued the Teutones. The Cimbri in particular also had the driving force of desperation – they had been wandering around Western Europe for well over a decade in search of a homeland. With all other prospects exhausted it was a case of Italy or bust. Either the itinerant nation would find a new home south of the Alps or the Cimbri as a people were doomed.

The Romans faced a similar existential challenge. They were not naive enough to believe that they and the Cimbri could ever peacefully co-exist in Italy. Given the warlike nature of the Cimbri and the expansionist nature of Rome, eventually the two very different cultures would end up fighting to the death, so the Romans reckoned they may as well start now. They had the advantage of better-trained and equipped infantry which were (for once) competently led. Unlike the invading force which basically now became two separate armies operating independently with almost no communication between them, the Romans in north

Italy had the advantage of interior lines of communication along well-established highways in terrain they knew well.

One negative factor, of which the Cimbri may or may not have been aware, was that Rome had been forced to open another front to its wars thanks to problems in the south. These problems were partly the result of pressure that the Cimbri were putting on Rome's empire as a whole, and partly due to the inherent flaws that were already pulling the Roman Republic apart.

Desperate for manpower, the Romans had called upon their allies for extra troops. This elicited a bitter response from the Bithynians whose lands had for years been subject to the merciless exactions of corrupt Roman authorities. Their king responded to the Roman request for men by pointing out that almost every able-bodied man in the kingdom had already been taken and enslaved by the Roman authorities for failure to meet the impossible demands of the tax collectors. (So hated did conduct such as this make the Romans that fifteen years later, when they got the chance, the people of Asia Minor rose up and killed every Roman or Italian they could find – some 80,000 of them.)

At present, the complaint of the Bithynians aroused something as near to shame as was possible for the Roman Senate. An edict was passed that those allied tax-debtors taken as slaves should be freed – and if possible, offered the chance to enlist. Sicily, at that time the breadbasket of Rome's growing empire, was particularly well-stocked with such slaves, who were treated in much the same manner as other agricultural livestock. When Nerva, the propraetor governing Sicily, obediently freed these men, he was greeted with a wave of rancorous resentment from the wealthy aristocrats who had owned them and simultaneously with huge discontent from those who remained slaves while others had been arbitrarily freed.

A desperate Nerva tried to put the genie back into the bottle by rescinding his decree, but desperate men who had once again tasted freedom were not planning to quietly return to bondage. They rebelled and were joined by those slaves still in servitude. Nerva sent a detachment of troops to put down the insurgency but his pitiful few hundred men were cut down by a mass of rebels now thousands strong and growing exponentially. The armour and weapons of the massacred Roman troops were gratefully taken up by the rebels, who eventually became a force of some 20,000 men – just what the Romans did not need when they already lacked the manpower to properly fight their northern war.

The threatened arrival of the Cimbri also caused other outbreaks of unrest elsewhere in Italy, for Roman arrogance and corruption meant that the city's rule was far from universally popular. Most of these, says the historian Diodorus Siculus (36.3), were 'short-lived and of little consequence', but a more serious outbreak occurred in southern Italy, where a somewhat-deranged Roman aristocrat set himself up as king of Campania and encouraged the slaves to revolt. This rebellion was controlled but the troops who did so were unavailable for the northern front, especially as thereafter they had to go south to deal with the even more severe threat in Sicily. Marius and Catulus were going to have to fight with what troops they had.

Marius had decided to begin his stand in Gaul at a large fortified camp near the modern city of Valence, building his fort on a hill which sloped gently north to south, overlooking the confluence of the Rhone and Isere rivers. Thanks to his canal, he had speedy access to the sea and supplies and also had a means to evacuate his army if he really had to. In keeping with his philosophy of only fighting when he wanted to, Marius made sure that his camp was fortified well enough to stand off the invading Teutones if they tried to take the place by storm, and stocked well enough to survive if the Teutones tried a siege.

(When Marius did this again in a later war, the frustrated enemy commander asked Marius 'If you are such a great general, why won't you come out and fight?' To which Marius replied. 'Well, if you think you are any good, why don't you try to make me?')

The Teutones took their time getting their army into position to confront Marius, quite possibly because they wanted to give the Cimbri as much time as possible to get into position on the other side of the Alps. It was probably already late summer when they moved to meet Marius with a huge army which crossed the left tributary of the Rhone and spread out in a mass of humanity which carpeted the plain for over a mile about the Roman camp.

The Teutones expected that Marius would march out to confront them in battle and the issue would be settled almost immediately. However, this did not happen, for the cautious Marius never rushed into that sort of thing. He informed the Roman legionaries that any man who wanted to rush out and engage the enemy would be considered a traitor rather than a hero.

Marius set the tone himself when a Teuton warrior came to the walls and challenged Marius to a personal duel, man to man. Perhaps recalling Scipio Africanus' famous reply to a similar challenge – that his mother had birthed a general, not a brawler – Marius merely told the man to go away and hang himself. When the fellow persisted, Marius produced a scrawny gladiator ('Near the end of his life' says Frontinus *Stratagems* 4.7.5) and suggested that he would be a more equal match for the Teuton. We have no record of what happened after this, but presumably the challenger retired in the face of the subsequent mockery from Marius' men.

Marius' men on the ramparts had been sent in detachments to stand guard and observe the enemy whom they would eventually have to fight. First, the men were instructed that they should get familiar with how the enemy operated in groups, what weapons they carried, and who their local leaders seemed to be. Not only did the Roman troops gain some basic military intelligence in this way, but more importantly they started to become accustomed to their enemy. As Plutarch put it:

Thus he [Marius] trained his men not to fear their size
nor cower at their war cries, strange and fierce though
these were ... and so in the course of time the strange and
ferocious was made to seem familiar. He thought that things
new were often given a quality of fearsomeness that only
existed in the imagination, but also even things which were
genuinely terrifying became less so after regular exposure.
And his legionaries not only became habituated to the sight
of their enemies but also the threats and boasts with which
the barbarian taunted them gradually drove them to fury.
(Plutarch, Marius 16)

Gradually the mood of the troops changed from fear of the
apparently unconquerable enemy to exasperation with Marius
for keeping them confined within the camp when the enemy
were right outside and waiting to engage. Marius screwed this
frustration up ever higher while denying that he was doing any
such thing. Instead, he informed the soldiers that his prophet had
discovered that the time was not yet ripe for an engagement. This
prophet was an eastern woman to whom Marius gave ostentatious
deference. It was claimed that the woman had presented herself
to the Roman Senate and offered to give them a quick preview of
how the war was going to go.

On being rejected by the senators, the prophet had joined the
wife of Marius as a spectator at a gladiator display, and amazed
the general's wife by confidently predicting the outcome of each
fight before it had even started. The wife sent the prophet to
Marius, who told the men that the gods had already arranged
a victory for Rome if only the crucial battle were fought at the
right time. In a further propaganda exercise, Marius encouraged
the taming of two vultures which had accompanied him on his
African campaign. Recognizable by the bronze rings which
circled their necks, these birds were considered as presaging a

victory for Marius when they appeared – as they miraculously did once again before the engagement with the Teutones. Whether these birds appeared from the god Jupiter, best and greatest, or from a cage hidden deep in the praetorian tent of Marius, the effect upon morale was the same.

Meanwhile, the usual signs and portents began to erupt across Italy as the population nervously awaited news of the battle which would decide their fate. Marius made sure the men heard all about one particular event, where a priest of the Magna Mater announced that the goddess had informed him that a great Roman victory was imminent. The Senate – who were also interested in raising public morale – decided to accept the prophecy and voted to build the goddess a temple to commemorate the victory. This so annoyed a sceptical Roman tribune that he denounced the priest as a fraud and physically attacked the man when he tried to address the people. What made the prophecy all the more credible was that the next day the disbelieving tribune was promptly smitten with a fever and died within the week.

Today we might dismiss all this as superstitious nonsense, forgetting that the men of Marius' army were well aware that it was mostly chance that would dictate whether they came through the following weeks without a foot or so of steel going through their guts. Under those circumstances men have a right to be superstitious, and it is a sign of Marius' ability as a general that he recognized that need and carefully used it to improve the morale of his army. If carefully selected omens predicted victory for Rome, Marius was more than happy to advertise the fact. He was well aware that before too long his army would find out for itself if the divine prophesies had been correct.

Chapter 8

The Battle of Aquae Sextae

When a Roman army on campaign made camp, this was more than just a place to spend the night. No Roman general willingly finished a day's march without setting up a fortified camp in a process which took several hours. Even if there was no immediate danger there remained good reasons for doing this. For a start, by and large the same camp was set up every night. Even if the army had marched twenty miles that day, that night each legionary bedded down with the same neighbours, the same distance between the command tent and the walls and the same route to the latrines. This gave individual soldiers a comforting sense of familiarity and stability no matter what was going on outside the walls – and even a Roman marching camp that would be occupied for only a few hours had walls.

The fact that a Roman army on the move made a point of digging up a defensive ditch and throwing up ramparts each night has delighted modern archaeologists as much as it annoyed Rome's enemies at the time. The main thing about such a camp was that it meant that a Roman army only need fight if the commander felt like doing so, because after centuries of constructing such field camps on a daily basis the Romans had become very good at it. In the case of Marius' camp on the banks of the Rhone, the army had dug in well in advance of the arrival of the Teutones and their defences were particularly good – especially since the Romans were facing an enemy who had little experience with siege warfare.

The result was predictable. Once the Teutones had got over their shock at what they loudly professed was the craven cowardice of the Romans, they settled down to testing the Roman defences and the morale of the soldiers manning them. This eventually escalated into an all-out attempt to storm the fortifications – exactly as Marius had hoped. The attackers were driven back by a storm of missiles, and these might also have constituted their first introduction to Roman heavy weaponry.

The Romans had been using a basic type of artillery called the *ballista* for at least the past fifty years. This basic torsion-spring weapon was something of a jack of all trades which could quickly be adapted to shoot either round stones at enemy walls or long arrow-like bolts at packed enemy infantry. It was also at around this time that we get the first references to a lighter version of the *ballista* called the scorpion. The scorpion was a specifically anti-personnel version of the *ballista*, adapted to use in the field rather than in a set-piece siege. If this weapon was available to Marius he would certainly have used it on this occasion, for he had been allowed plenty of time to prepare his defences and had his custom-built canal to bring in whatever supplies he wanted from Rome.

For the attacking Teutones it must have been a demoralizing experience to have these heavy weapons tearing through their close-packed ranks, passing unstoppably through shields and bodies alike. Then, once the assault had come within hand-thrown missile range, the attackers discovered again what a devastating weapon a well-flung *pilum* could be. The Teutones persevered with their attack on the camp for three days (says the historian Osorius) before deciding that their direct assault had been a dismal failure that left behind a significant number of casualties. Even more important, this first setback had demonstrated to Roman and Teuton alike that the barbarian army was not the unstoppable force it had been advertised as being. In the right circumstances a Roman army could hold its own while simultaneously hurting the enemy.

The next step for the Teutones was to settle down around the Roman camp – after all, they had Marius trapped behind the walls of his fort – and eventually he would have to come out and face their overwhelming numbers. Yet it was those same overwhelming numbers that were the problem. Marius had prepared his camp with care and made sure that it had both access to water and plentiful foodstuffs stashed within. The massive Teuton army had not arrived expecting a siege and was largely living off the land, a strategy that only worked if the land provided enough to live on. Within a very short time the Teutones had exhausted all the food available locally and needed to move on, whether they wanted to or not.

While the Teuton leaders were doubtless unhappy at leaving a competent army at large behind them, they had little choice but to continue their advance into Italy. The one advantage of living off the land was that at least they had no lines of communication for Marius to cut, though the Teutones were certainly aware that any retreat from Italy was likewise blocked. Therefore, now doubly committed, the Teutones broke camp and recommenced their march on Rome. The breaking of the Teuton camp was apparently done in instalments, possibly in the hope that the diminishing number of his opponents might encourage Marius to launch an attack. The other alternative is to take Plutarch literally and assume that the number of the enemy was so great that their column of march really did take six days to pass by the Roman camp.

Certainly, the annoyed Teutones were in no hurry to go and loudly informed the Romans on the walls of their intentions towards the legionaries' wives and daughters once they reached Italy. They insultingly enquired whether those on the walls had any last messages that they wanted passed to the doomed families whom the Teutones would soon be seeing.

As soon as the last of the enemy had gone by, Marius also broke camp and set off after them. Yet again, he was always careful to construct a strong marching camp at the end of every day, so if the Teutones did turn upon the army shadowing them they would once again be frustrated by those unyielding Roman walls. (In fact, the Teutones had learned from bitter experience and never even tried.) Once again the sheer number of his enemy was turned by Marius to his advantage, for the unwieldy mass of the Teutones made their army much slower than his own – especially as this was the new, meaner, leaner version of the Roman army that Marius had spent the past few years developing. So not only did Marius have time to construct a complete marching camp at the end of every day, sometimes he even pulled level with the Teutones and camped alongside them.

This from the Roman viewpoint was again good for morale, since the Roman legionaries could be persuaded that they were now actually pursuing their enemy. The presence of the Roman army also greatly inconvenienced the Teutones because an army living off the land needs to forage, and a large army needs to forage a lot. With Roman skirmishers and cavalry constantly harassing isolated groups, foraging could only be done in strength, and with the Teutones moving into unfriendly territory, supplies were getting harder to come by as peasants hustled their livestock out of the way.

We can assume that the two armies followed the ancient road alongside the Rhone as far as the Massilot city of the Avenionsios (Avignon) before turning eastward towards the Piedmontese Alps. By now the duelling forces were in territory which the Romans knew well and it is possible that Marius had already selected his battleground for the decisive clash. The question is whether that battleground was where the battle actually took place. There is an element of spontaneity about the final confrontation with the Teutones that – for all Plutarch's later rationalizing – suggests that things did not go according to plan.

The clash came at Aquae Sextae, near the modern city of Aix-en-Provence, well over a hundred miles from the point where Marius had first met the Teutones. One effect of Marius' methodical harassment of the invading force was that it had split along ethnic lines, probably so that each group could forage more effectively. Though they were still close to each other, the fact that there were two parts of the barbarian army offered Marius the tantalizing prospect of being able to take on each part separately. If we go with this theory then the logical first target would be the Ambrones, for this tribal grouping, though an alleged 30,000 strong, was only a fraction of the size of the main Teuton force. Accordingly, Marius camped alongside the Ambrones and waited for his opportunity.

If Marius had decided that this was where he intended to make his stand, the location was not a bad one, for he had nearby the Roman settlement of Aquae Sextae. This town either had the six springs which its name implies, or was named after the Roman praetor Sextius Calvinus, who had founded the place twenty years previously. Several trade routes passed nearby, for the town was located at a natural choke point for east-west communications. If defeated in the coming clash, the Romans could retreat within the town's walls for at least temporary refuge.

Once again Marius had decided to camp near the Ambrones, in a strong position uphill from a river – probably the River Arc. It was an excellent location with one major drawback – the nearest water was that river, and the water was already being used by the Ambrones. In fact, some of the tribesmen had discovered that there were a number of natural hot springs near the river and were taking the opportunity to enjoy the hot baths provided by Mother Nature. According to Plutarch, Marius had deliberately chosen to make a dry camp in order to give his men an incentive to fight, as they evidently were going to have to do if they wanted access to the water. On the other hand, according to the

Stratagems of Frontinus (who was more of a military man than the very unwarlike Plutarch) the location of the Roman camp was a blunder by the Roman engineers who located it there. (Frontinus, *Stratagems* 2.4.6)

Marius had probably also not foreseen that the Ambrones would be enjoying the hot water so much that they made access to the river difficult. It would be very out of character for the cautious Marius to deliberately select a position where his army might be discombobulated through thirst, especially as this meant that he would be unable to have in reserve his usual option of being able to stand siege in his camp. Indeed, that caution showed again when his men asked if they could drive off the Ambrones who were blocking access to the river water 'before their blood dried up' (says Plutarch, histrionically). Marius' reply was 'After we have fortified the camp.'

While the legionaries settled down to their customary task of preparing ditches and ramparts, some of the camp servants decided to take unilateral action. The camp mules needed water and the servants could not prepare meals without it. So, a large group of men took up their water jars, and axes and cudgels also, and set out for the river determined to get water even if they had to fight for it.

If this was Marius' way of starting a battle it was certainly an odd one, and seems more the manner that a battle might start by chance, as had – to choose one of many examples – the Battle of Cynoscephalae in Greece, almost a century previously. There, as now, a chance encounter between elements of the rival armies resulted in a clash from which neither side would back down. Instead, both sides kept feeding units into the fray until it became clear that a major clash was inevitable.

In this case, the startled Ambrones at the river called for help from their comrades in the main camp. Clearly these men also had no idea that battle was about to be joined for many of them had already eaten, and in some cases even opened the first casks of wine for the evening. (Plutarch, *Marius* 19) Nevertheless, if battle there was to be, the Ambrones were quite prepared to accept the challenge. While skirmishing continued along the river, the main army methodically prepared to push back the impertinent Roman servants as an organized body. Once armed, the Ambrones formed a proper battle line and marched down to clear the riverbank. Swords or spears were banged against shields in a set pattern and when the rhythm reached a particular point the entire army shouted their tribal name, 'Ambrones!', and leapt forward.

Either all was going perfectly to Marius' plan, or at this point the Roman general realized that he had a perfect opportunity to defeat one segment of the enemy army by itself. It was by now late enough in the evening for it to be impossible for the main body of the Teutones to get organized and march to join the Ambrones before night fell. Furthermore, if the Ambrones did defeat the Romans, Marius still had the option of falling back on his camp, albeit with thirsty and demoralized soldiers.

However, at present the problem was more that his soldiers were, if anything, too keen to engage the enemy whose taunts and threats had been getting them increasingly annoyed. None were more annoyed than the Ligurian cohorts in the Roman army. These people were almost locals, for Liguria occupies the arc known today as the Italian Riviera where the top of the Italian peninsula meets France, less than 100km from Aquae Sextae. The Ligurians had a historical connection with the name 'Ambrones' and still claimed it for themselves. (The *ambr-* root is common to several Indo-European names and does not necessarily suggest any blood relationship between the two groups. For example, the people of modern Umbria in south-central Italy probably once had the same name.) Nevertheless, the Ligurians took exception to 'their' name being chanted by the barbarian army and quickly formed ranks to defend their national honour.

The result was a somewhat childish shouting match with the two sides advancing upon one another, each trying to outdo the other by bellowing the name more ferociously than the other side. Meanwhile, the rest of the Roman army were being frantically mustered into battle order, for if this was all part of a cunning Marian scheme, no-one had bothered to tell the centurions and junior officers who actually had to get the men ready for combat. Indeed, at this point Plutarch abandons the master-plan thesis and admits that 'So then, the story goes that the battle on the riverbank came about by accident rather than through the careful machinations of the general.'

Nevertheless, things worked out fortuitously for Rome (or, as Marius doubtless reported later, with exquisite timing), for the Ligurians reached the riverbank just as the first of the Ambrones were crossing. The Ligurians were too few to prevent the Ambrones from getting across the river, but numerous enough to ensure that those enemies who did cross arrived on the other side disorganized and out of battle formation. Then, with half of the army of the Ambrones on one side of the river and the other half struggling to form ranks on the Roman side, six legions of Roman infantry came storming downhill in perfect formation. The Ambrones already across the river could not resist the Roman charge, but since they were already with their backs to the river they could not easily retreat either. The result was brutal, messy, and finished with the river water too polluted with blood to be drinkable anyway. Very little of that blood was Roman.

Like the good general that he was, Marius pressed his attack mercilessly and pushed his army across the river without giving the surviving Ambrones the chance to reform. The Ambrones had by now lost their appetite for a fight in any case and were streaming back to camp while the Romans chopped them down from behind. When they reached the waggons which the tribe customarily drew up as a defensive wall around their camp, the warriors discovered another problem – their women.

The women of the Ambrones were in little doubt of their fate should their camp fall to the Romans. The rules of war at that time made the occupants of a captured camp subject to whatever the conquerors wanted, and many of the women of the Ambrones were quite prepared to face death if the alternative was rape and slavery. Armed with axes and camp tools they threw themselves at the tide of struggling humanity coming their way and tried with prayers and curses to get their menfolk facing in the right direction. They also tried to pull away the shields of the attacking Romans and even grabbed at their swords, probably aware that the legionaries might be more gentle with them than with the warriors – not out of any sense of chivalry but so as not to harm human livestock that they might have a use for later.

In the event, the women would have been wiser to flee, for the Romans were in no position to follow up their victory. Instead, as Plutarch reports:

> Although they had slaughtered many of the Ambrones, the Romans retreated as night fell. Usually after such a victory the men sing hymns of triumph while downing celebratory drinks in their tents, or talk with their comrades over a hearty dinner before enjoying that sweetest of pleasures after a battle fought and won – a solid night's sleep.
>
> Not in this case. The night was filled with fears and alarms, for [the sudden onset of battle meant that] the army's camp still had no rampart or ditch, and there remained the threat of tens of thousands of the enemy still undefeated, not to mention those Ambrones who had escaped in the earlier clash.... Marius himself was in a state of some agitation as he struggled to prepare his men for the chaos and confusion of a night battle. (Plutarch, *Marius* 20)

Such a battle seemed imminent because the Teutones and surviving Ambrones were not taking their defeat at all well.

> The entire plain was filled with a terrifying racket, not just the wails and groans one might expect, but howls of grief and bellowed threats that seemed almost bestial. Coming from so vast a multitude the sound filled the river valley and echoed off the hills around. (Plutarch, *Marius* 20)

The Romans remained stood-to in their ranks all night, awaiting the vengeance of Teutobod's army. With the dawn some men could be relieved and work began upon the belated reinforcement of the camp's defences. Meanwhile, careful reconnaissance by scouts confirmed that the Teutones were readying for battle, although this did not appear to be imminent. Marius was well aware that eventually the Teutones would be coming for revenge and that, as the defending party, he could choose where to meet their advance.

We have a rough description of the battleground. The Teutones were encamped at the bottom of a gentle slope cut by ditches, possibly created by erosion, with trees on each side. To one side, nearer Marius' camp, the slope levelled out to become a more open plain. After careful study of the situation, Marius decided that he would offer battle by drawing up his army right at the top of the slope where he could pin his exposed flank with his camp. His cavalry would be useless in the tight confines of the battleground that he hoped to create, so he sent them to contain any of the enemy who spilled out on to the plain on that side of the battle line.

Unusually for a Roman general, Marius sent his officers fanning out through the ranks to explain his reasoning to the men. The legionaries would have been told that, firstly, by waiting just outside his camp Marius had ensured that the enemy would have to come to him, which involved climbing in full armour up the rough slope between the two camps. Secondly, because the Romans were lined up on the crest of the slope, the enemy would still be fighting uphill when they arrived, and as Marius made sure his legionaries were aware, the enemy's javelins would have little reach and their blows would lack force.

Because of the trees lining each side of the slope, the Teutones would be forced into a narrow battle line, where the Roman skill at organized close combat would give them a local advantage. Ideally, the Teutones could be held at the top of the slope and then forced backwards so that they were moving downhill on ground that – because of the ditches – offered treacherous footing.

What Marius did not want was for enough of the enemy to force their way past the unpinned flank of his army and form up on the open ground available there, as this would make him fight on the more level ground of the plain. Marius had stationed his cavalry against that very eventuality, but cavalry would be relatively useless if the Teutones kept their battle line in place as they expanded their flank to take in this more advantageous position. However, if the battle came to that, Marius had other surprises in store.

Much depended on the Teutones being so hell-bent on revenge that they would ignore the tactical advantages which Marius had arranged for the benefit of his army and attack nevertheless, relying upon their ferocity and vastly superior numbers to carry the day. Indeed, it could hardly have turned out differently, for King Teutobod would hardly maintain his prestige among his people if he appeared afraid of an army of – at most – some 35,000 men when he had somewhere between five and nine times that number.

The problem was, as the Teutones discovered after they had charged up the slope, that only a fraction of their army could engage with the narrow Roman front at one time. Meanwhile, those lining up behind for their turn to get at the Romans had to deal with a steady hail of *pila* which back-ranking legionaries could throw downhill with deadly effect. Marius' men were by now well-rested, and their morale was fortified by the memory of their recent defeat of the Ambrones. All the Romans had to do for the moment was to hold their ground with locked shields and use their vicious, short stabbing swords to deadly effect upon an enemy too packed in their front ranks to use their own longer slashing weapons effectively.

Eventually as the day wore on, the Teutones managed to force their way on to the open ground of the plain, where they had more room to manoeuvre and were at least fighting on level ground. Having finally gained this position, there followed a brief pause while the Teutones and legions re-arranged their ranks in light of the new situation.

Barely had the battle lines re-engaged when total chaos broke out at the rear of the Teuton force. A large detachment of mixed Roman infantry and cavalry came pouring out of concealment in the trees and fell upon the backs of the enemy. This was all the more shocking to the Teuton leadership because they were no fools and had carefully estimated the size of the Roman forces that they were facing. There was no way that Marius could have mustered a force of the size now attacking from the rear, so where had these men come from? Confusion at the top did little to quell growing panic among the men on the ground, and as soon as the Teutones hesitated, the Romans charged.

Morale among the Teutones was already softening after their army's failure to make much impression on the Roman lines in the initial attack. Now the entry into the battle of a totally unexpected new force – attacking at their most vulnerable point – caused those with a clear line of escape to head off the battlefield. Once the first men started running, others joined in and the entire Teuton force collapsed in rout.

This was just as well, because the large detachment of Roman soldiers attacking from the rear was in fact a small detachment of Roman soldiers making a lot of noise. Had they stopped to examine these attackers more carefully, the confused Teutones might have noticed that the majority of these 'legionaries' were actually servants, grooms and camp-followers, all aggressively waving spears behind a thin front rank of genuine legionaries. Nor did those threatening lines of cavalry fall upon the fleeing men or the exposed backs of those still fighting. This was not because their discipline was holding them steady, but because they were not cavalry at all. Rather they were pack-mules and donkeys tricked out in cavalry saddle cloths with just enough genuine horses among them to pass muster at first glance – which is all that most Teutones gave them before bolting for safety. (Frontinus, *Stratagems* 2.4.6)

The Teuton leaders who survived the battle might justifiably have been outraged when they discovered how they had been tricked. Until this point Marius had appeared to be a known quality – he was a conservative, risk-averse general who only fought when he had the odds in his favour and had given himself a secure line of retreat. That he should turn the battle upon an outlandish stratagem was something which had literally not occurred to them. If it had, the Teuton leaders would have sent scouts to check out the treeline with greater care.

As it was, this oversight not only cost the Teutones the battle but also ended their part in the war. In a battle of this sort casualties are comparatively light, for men with relatively inefficient swords or spears are stabbing at opponents bearing armour, shields and helmets. These men are actively defending themselves and have usually had a reasonable amount of experience or at least practice at doing so. As a result, despite a morning of hewing, stabbing and getting stabbed all along the battle line, the 35,000 men of the Roman army suffered less than a thousand killed or wounded.

On the other hand, when an army broke and turned to rout, the casualties were horrendous. One of the major functions of cavalry in these circumstances was to hit the fleeing enemy hard, cutting down from behind near-defenceless men as they fled, often after these men had abandoned shield and sword. The only way to prevent this slaughter by the cavalry was for men to gather into defensive groups, which the cavalry swerved around while seeking easier prey. The defensive groups could be left to face their next problem – an organized army advancing at speed which would demolish these *ad hoc* formations as easily as a wave overrunning a sandcastle on the beach.

Consequently, once their line was broken, the Teuton warriors were doomed whether they stood and fought against the oncoming legions or fled before the merciless cavalry. Their only hope was to reach the shelter of those woods from which the Roman ambush had so recently erupted, and where the trees would slow down the Roman horsemen. Some men managed this, including King Teutobad, but they were a minority. An estimated 3,000 Teutones escaped from the battlefield with another 50,000 or so captured and at least 100,000 slain. The numbers are a rough estimate because no-one at the time was counting. The nearest contemporary account comes from a summary of Livy (*Periochae* 68) which gives the remarkably high figure of 200,000 slain and 90,000 captured, which at least approximates to the original figure of an army of 300,000 men.

Whatever the exact and now-unknowable casualty figures, the main issue was whether the Teutones remained as a force in the war, which they did not. At Aquae Sextae the Teuton fighting force was effectively destroyed. Plutarch recounts that for years afterwards the bones of the fallen warriors were used by the locals to fence their vineyards, and that 'after the corpses had rotted away into the soil, and the winter rains had fallen upon it, the earth became so rich in putrefied matter that it yielded stupendous harvests year after year.' (Plutarch, *Marius* 21)

After their experience with the women of the Ambrones, the Romans approached the camp of the Teutones with some circumspection. After all, there was a lot of human booty therein that no-one wanted to damage. For what happened next we have a reference from – of all people – St Jerome of Jerusalem, who wrote some 450 years later of the fate of the captured high-born ladies of the Teuton force.

> Some three hundred of these women faced capture by the Romans. When they realized this they first implored the consul that they might be allowed to serve the Romans as priestesses or temple servants in the temples of Ceres and Venus. (Jerome, 123.8)

Sadly, Marius felt no need at all to take these women's feelings into consideration, and may have reminded them of the coarse indignities which the Teuton warriors had promised for the women of Rome as they marched past his earlier camp. Then he ordered his lictors to remove the supplicants.

> Realizing that their case was hopeless, they killed their little children and strangled each other during the night. They were found the next morning all dead in one another's arms. (Jerome 123.8)

The historian Orosius (writing at an equally late date) confirms this story, differing from Jerome only in that he claims the women wanted to become servants of Vesta, and that swords as well as nooses were used in the subsequent mass suicide. (Orosius, History 5.16ff)

These later historians also differ upon the fate of King Teutobod, with Orosius claiming that he perished along with his men, and another late source, Florus (*Epitome* 1.38), claiming that the king was later captured and because of his height made a striking figure in Marius' subsequent triumphal procession. 'The man who could vault over four, or even six horses at once, could not find a horse swift enough to carry him to safety', gloats Florus, who also feels that in the battle the midday heat caused the bodies of the northerners to melt like snow – notwithstanding that these northerners had by now spent several summers in Gaul.

That sojourn in Gaul now came back to haunt those Teutones who escaped the massacre at Aquae Sextae. After enduring over a year of pillage and massacre by the Teuton horde, the Gauls were hardly sympathetic towards the remnants of the defeated army. An unknown number of escapees from the battlefield were quietly slaughtered wherever the Gauls discovered them, while a group of around 1,000 Teutones, including several of their former leaders, was discovered by the Sequani tribe, who took great pleasure in handing them over to the Romans. (It goes without saying that, after Aquae Sextae, Roman prestige in the region had rebounded with meteoritic speed.) Only a tiny number of survivors escaped to make their way around the Alps to bring the dire news to Boiorix and his Cimbric army.

Just as the victory over the Ambrones had not granted the Romans relief so much as further anxiety about what the other half of the enemy army would do, so the overall victory at Aquae Sextae removed only one problem. Before anyone could think of celebrating, there remained the other threat to Italy – the army of the Cimbri now descending upon northeastern Italy. This army was just as large as the army of the Teutones and Ambrones, and contained more seasoned warriors, all desperate to find a homeland. Against them stood the less-well-trained army of Catulus, who, whatever other fine qualities he may have possessed, was not in Marius' class as a general. The battle for Italy was by no means over.

Chapter 9

The War in the Northeast

With the Teuton force obliterated, Marius gave his army a few moments in which to regain its collective breath. Some of this time was spent in the usual post-battle occupation of looting the tents and corpses of the defeated. This was a profitable business, for the Teutones had by this time spent several years pillaging their way down from Scandinavia and had amassed a fine collection of booty. This booty, Plutarch says, the men of the army collectively voted to turn over to Marius out of gratitude that he had actually led them to victory – in stark contrast to every other Roman general, who in marching out to deal with the northern threat had led his men to the slaughter.

This raises the question of why Marius had succeeded so brilliantly where his predecessors had failed. One reason is certainly that Marius was simply a better commander than his predecessors. Whereas earlier generals had operated on the basic principle that their job was to locate the enemy and point the Roman army at them, Marius had gone much further. He showed great (and un-Roman) restraint in not attempting to give battle upon contact with the enemy, but instead gave his men time to become accustomed to the sight and conduct of the men whom they would be fighting.

Marius then showed that he could seize an opportunity when it presented itself, as it did when the Ambrones gave him a chance to destroy their portion of the army without the Teutones being able to reinforce them in time. Then, when it came time to dispose of the Teutones, Marius carefully arranged matters so that the greatest advantages of the enemy were negated. Their huge numbers were funnelled into a narrow battlefield and their ferocious charge was blunted by the slope up which it had to be executed. Finally, Marius showed considerable foresight and ingenuity by anticipating that the Teutones would eventually be able to force their way on to the plain and arranging there the surprise attack on their rear by a large force which Marius did not, in fact, possess.

Yet, before we dismiss Marius' predecessors as merely incompetent aristocratic fools (though we should allow that definition to stand in the case of Servilius Caepio), it must be remembered that Marius had the benefit of ten years of their experience of how not to fight the Cimbri. Thus Marius knew, for example, that he had to cancel out that first, overwhelming charge, simply because the Romans had seen at first hand what would happen if they did not. He also knew that the sheer number of the enemy force meant that it had to keep moving, and therefore any well-provisioned camp capable of withstanding siege was secure because the enemy could not take the camp before they began to starve. All the lessons which the Romans had learned the hard way were applied by Marius in the Aquae Sextae campaign.

Furthermore, the army which Marius took north was one which Rutilius Rufus had been carefully training exclusively for that purpose, though it is to Marius' great credit that he saw what else had to be done and ruthlessly altered the structure of his army so that it was capable of doing it. Thus, for example, the leaner Roman army of 'Marian mules' was able to move faster than the unwieldy mass of the Teuton host and find a safe place to camp next to the enemy every night on the long march from the Rhone to the site of the battlefield at Aquae Sextae. Finally, Marius had the benefit of an espionage network which the Romans had been quietly building up over the past years.

We mainly know of this network because the enterprising young officer Sertorius had joined it for a while after Arausio. Before then the matter was barely mentioned because the Romans regarded spying upon the enemy as somewhat distasteful and were loath to admit that they did it rather well. Nevertheless, we do know that the Romans had a number of spies in the enemy camp, mainly in the form of Gallic auxiliaries. These men would have been all the more effective because the rough democracy of the northern tribes meant that the leaders discussed many of their decisions in public meetings with their warriors. So Marius would have had the advantage of knowing where and when his opponents would be moving and for what purpose.

All these elements came together in the Aquae Sextae campaign, to which Plutarch supplies us with the perfect cinematic finish.

Once the battle was done, Marius selected from the armour and other booty taken from the barbarians such items as were intact, splendid and suitable for display in his forthcoming triumphal procession. All the rest of the barbarian equipment he piled up to make a huge pyre on which he intended to sacrifice to the gods in grand style. [And, not incidentally, to make sure the local tribesmen did not pick up enough military gear to equip several armies.]

The soldiers formed up about the pyre in battle array, but bearing wreaths upon their heads. Marius was clad in a purple robe [signifying a victorious general] and had taken the torch with which to personally light the fire. As he ritually raised the torch in both hands towards the heavens some horsemen were seen galloping towards them. The riders were greeted by total silence as everyone waited to see what their arrival portended. The newcomers were seen to be friendly, and as they reached Marius they dismounted and greeted him with the happy news that [in his absence] the people of Rome had made him consul for the fifth time. They then passed over the official documentation to that effect.

The soldiers were wildly enthusiastic [because this meant that Marius would be their commander for another year] and deemed this a further cause of celebration to be added to their victory. They greeted the news with a great shout accompanied by the clash of their arms against their shields. The officers then crowned Marius afresh with a bay wreath [significant because a wreath from the bay laurel tree – *Laurus nobilis* – indicated that the wearer had earned a Roman triumph] and thereafter Marius lit the pyre and completed the sacrifice. (Plutarch, *Marius 22*)

That wrapped up events in the northwest. Marius next doubtless sat down with the newcomers to discuss news of what the Cimbri had been doing and how Catulus and his army were faring in the war against this even-larger and more-threatening enemy who had now reached the northeast of Italy. (Unlike Marius, Catulus had not been re-elected as consul, a job which went to a nonentity called Manius Aquillius. However, there was considerable civil strife in Rome at this time due to fears of the oncoming Cimbric onslaught and the activities of the unscrupulous Saturninus. The Senate felt, with good reason, that at least one consul was needed to keep a grip of things in the city itself, and therefore Catulus remained in charge of his army as a proconsul.)

Very little is known of the march of the Cimbri across the base of the Alps and how they fared in their travels before they reached Italy. Most accounts of what happened begin with a description of how Catulus tried, and failed, to prevent the Cimbri from forcing the high alpine passes. Nevertheless, getting around the northern Alps could not have been an easy march for the Cimbri. Certainly, the fact that they were just passing through would have helped tribes such as the Helveti to tolerate their passing, and it was late enough in the year for the Cimbri to be able to help themselves to the harvests of the lands through which they passed.

Nevertheless, with winter approaching local tribes very much wanted those harvests for themselves and would at the least have parted reluctantly with their crops. Added to Cimbric difficulties was the fact that the mountainous terrain of modern Switzerland and the Tyrol does not lend itself easily to mass migration. But it does make for easy defence by stubborn tribesmen who knew that the Cimbri were a tribe in a hurry who simply did not have the time to storm every defended mountain pass. The Cimbric march must have seen both messy combat and extensive diplomacy by Boiorix to make it possible for his horde to have reached Italy before the winter set in.

At what time the Cimbri did arrive in Italy is a matter of some controversy. The only chronological reference we have is by the late historian Florus, who assures us that the horde arrived *per heimem* – in winter. This is dubious, but it is certainly possible that the Cimbri cleared the passes just as the first snows were falling.

The description of what happened next must be treated with some caution because it is probably derived from two more-than-somewhat biased sources. One of these sources is Catulus himself, for it is known that he wrote an account of the campaign called the *Liber de consulatu et rebus gestis suis* (*The Book of his Consulship and Matters Related Thereto*). This was used as a source by those later Roman historians whose work has survived to the present day, unlike the original book of which only three small fragments remain.

The other of these sources was by another of the Roman commanders in the Cimbric wars, an up-and-coming aristocrat called Cornelius Sulla. This work also has not survived, but we know it was referred to extensively by Plutarch who provides us with the best description of the war. Sulla was, like Catulus, a Roman aristocrat whose family had suffered political decline.

Sulla was determined to reverse that decline and his energy and competence had recommended him to Marius who appointed Sulla as one of his senior officers in the Jugurthine War. Sulla had done well in that war and it was his coolness under pressure and his smooth negotiating skills which had led to the capture of Jugurtha himself. The success of his subordinate had irked Marius, who was not fond of sharing the limelight with anyone else. Therefore in recent years Sulla and his former commander had drifted apart to the extent that when the war with the Cimbri again became urgent, Sulla chose to enrol with Catulus rather than Marius.

There are hints that in late 102 Sulla first engaged with the Tigurini who had accompanied the Cimbri on their alpine trek. If so, these operations were more successful than other Roman activities in northeast Italy, for the Tigurini took no further part in the campaign. Indeed, the only further reference to them is as 'contemptible refugees and bandits' who eventually left Italy of their own accord.

Thereafter Sulla took over the job of securing the loyalty of the tribes inhabiting the Alpine regions which the Cimbri would be crossing, and simultaneously extracting from these regions supplies to send to the main army of his commander. This was a task well suited to a man with skills at organization and diplomacy, and Sulla allegedly did an excellent job (even though there is good reason for suspecting that the ultimate source for this praise was the history written by Sulla himself). The army of Catulus, which had previously been somewhat short of provisions, now found itself living in plenty – and indeed Sulla was even able to divert some of this abundance to the Marian army.

We can be pretty sure that Plutarch was not drawing upon the memoirs of Catulus when he describes that commander's initial reaction to the Cimbric advance as 'sluggish'. Given that the destination of the horde had been known for months, it would be expected that Catulus would take the obvious step of holding the Cimbri at the Alpine passes. Some of these passes remain challenging even today, and even the wider passes such as the Predil Pass are considerably more defensible than the open plain of the Veneto and the Po valley below.

Either Catulus was uncertain which passes the Cimbri intended to use – from Roman accounts we know the Cimbric plan was to arrive 'by way of Noricum'. However, this geographic designation is vague enough to allow wide latitude. Alternatively, Catulus was also reluctant to divide his forces (says Plutarch). In all he had some 20,000 men, which is not a lot with which to cope with several hundred thousand Cimbri, their allies, and alpine tribesmen of dubious loyalty.

If Catulus put all his eggs in one basket and defended a single pass, the Cimbri could use two or more – there are a host of minor passes in the region. The last thing Catulus would want was to have the Cimbri cross by several passes and then get between him and his supply lines, leaving him stranded in the high Alps. Yet the alternative was to split his army and hope that detachments of a few thousand men could hold out in their individual passes, Thermopylae-style, against overwhelming odds. In a way, Catulus was doomed to fail whichever option he selected, and fail he duly did. The only description of this initial aspect of the campaign is a laconic summary of Livy: 'They [the Cimbri] drove the proconsul Q. Catulus back from his attempt to block the Alps and put him to flight.' (*Epitome* 68)

Livy is useful because elsewhere he mentions that one of Catulus' defensive positions was on the River Atesis, (the modern Adige) which would suggest that at least one entry point of the Cimbri was through the Reschen Pass, which today connects the Austrian Tyrol with the Val Venosa region. Another point of entry therefore may have been the Brenner Pass somewhat to the east.

With this information, we can consider Catulus' failed strategy as follows. His military intelligence would have informed him that the Cimbri would not be coming as far east as the Veneto, making the upper valley of the Adige the logical point of entry. Catulus could therefore attempt to challenge the Cimbri while they were still tired out from their arduous transit of the Alps, or remain in the plain while his enemies got their act together.

This second option would have involved falling back on Cremona and probably waiting for the spring to recommence operations. Thereafter Catulus would have had to hope that he could keep his much smaller force – apparently a standard consular army of two legions plus auxilia – from being outmanoeuvred and overwhelmed by the sheer weight of Cimbric numbers. Catulus decided to grasp the nettle and advance, correctly reasoning that if he was thrown back from the Alps, fighting on the plains remained as option B. At least by advancing up the Adige he had the river pinning one flank and the mountains the other.

Why this strategy failed we do not know – possibly the Cimbri did use multiple passes, in which case Catulus would have to retreat before he was cut off. He did leave behind a cohort guarding one fort and the fate of that garrison is somewhat confused. By one tradition, related by Plutarch, the men fought off the advancing Cimbri for several days. They were eventually forced to surrender on terms – those terms being that they were allowed to depart once they had sworn upon the idol of a bronze bull that they would take no further part in the war. By another account, the men staged a breakout and re-joined the army of Catulus on their own terms.

To confuse matters further, there followed a similar situation later, and what happened on which of these occasions is something which even later Roman historians appear to have had difficulty sorting out. However, it is to that later occasion that we now turn, for we note that whoever summarized Livy at this point was certainly trying to be sparing with words. Therefore, we can assume that the sentence 'They [the Cimbri] drove the proconsul Q. Catulus back from his attempt to block the Alps and put him to flight,' refers to two separate events. The 'driving back' occurred when Catulus tried to block the passes, and the 'putting to flight' happened on a subsequent occasion.

That subsequent occasion happened because, rather than fall all the way back to Cremona, Catulus dug in to make a stand further down the Adige at Tridentum. (It should be noted that references to 'Tridentum' are slightly anachronistic, since at this point we are looking at a small Rhaetian town that was only formally made the Roman settlement of Tridentum in later decades. It is now the city of Trento.) Plutarch gives us a wonderful and highly dubious description of the conduct of the Cimbri as they followed the retreating Catulus, and this is worth repeating if only for the mental images it evokes.

> The barbarians held their enemies in contempt and followed them boldly. They endured snowstorms naked, not because they had to, but as a way of displaying their courage and fortitude. They would make their way through ice and deep snow to the peaks, and once there would put their wide shields beneath them and let themselves go sliding over the smooth snow past the ravines. (Plutarch, *Marius* 23)

Catulus must have retreated from the tobogganing Cimbri down the western bank of the Adige, this being the only option because the terrain across the river is unsuitable for the movement of a large army. For the same reason, the Cimbri must have followed along the same route. When it did become possible to cross the Adige, somewhere below Tridentum, Catulus did so, knowing that the Cimbri would have to cross the river to get to him. From this location Catulus could control access to the Italian plain both through the valley of the Adige and also the Valle Iscaro. His problem was that if he moved his entire army onto the east bank of the river, the Cimbri could choose to ignore him altogether and continue down the other bank of the Adige into the Veneto by way of where Verona stands today.

To prevent this, Catulus built a double camp, with his main army on the east bank and a smaller but heavily fortified camp on the west. The reasoning behind this strategy seems fairly straightforward. The Cimbri could not ignore a strong position directly to their rear, especially as later evidence would indicate that this fortification contained a substantial number of cavalry. Catulus had linked the camps on each side of the river by a sturdy bridge so that when the time came that the Cimbri – as they must – tried to storm the west bank fort, Catulus could feed men and materiel across the river as needed. In short, he envisaged a siege without the main problem of a siege, which is the lack of a secure line of supply for the besieged. Furthermore, Catulus would have been as aware as Marius had been that his opponents were far from expert at siege warfare.

While the Cimbri were no experts at siege warfare, they were not fools either. There is little doubt that Cimbric spies had the Romans under observation from the moment they marched up the Adige valley, and they would have studied Catulus innovative double camp with interest. The critical part of this camp was the bridge and this, given Cimbric ingenuity, was also the weakest part.

> After they made camp by the river and examined the crossing they began to dam up the water. Like the giants of legend they began tearing apart the nearby hills and ripping chunks out of the nearby cliffs. They carried into the river whole trees with their roots, and then sent the whole heavy mass downstream where it went tumbling against the piles of the bridge. (Plutarch *Marius* 23)

Either the intent here was to break the bridge – although Plutarch rather annoyingly does not tell us if that happened – or the massive amount of debris threatening to take down the structure was a side effect caused by a failed attempt by the Cimbri to cross to Catulus' side of the river by building a dam across it. In either case the threat to the bridge was enough to rouse in the Romans in the smaller camp an urgent desire to be with their comrades in the east-bank camp before the bridge collapsed. At this point a chaotic situation had developed – the Romans in the smaller camp were in a state of confused retreat across the bridge and at the same time they may have faced the prospect of an imminent or even simultaneous Cimbric attack. (Plutarch confusingly calls the smaller west-bank camp the 'main' camp, but this may have been a reference to that camp's greater strategic importance, rather than its size.)

This seems to have been the moment when yet another of the Roman aristocracy displayed the sort of military ability which had led to the Roman people deciding to reject the entire class as commanders and select Marius instead. The villain in this case was Aemilius Scaurus, the son of the veteran general whom most of Rome suspected of having been bribed by Jugurtha in the African War. When the Cimbri attacked, the younger Scaurus apparently decided that all was lost and fled with the cavalry to the safety of 'the city' – be that city Tridentum or Rome.

The exact context of this precipitate desertion is unknown, for one source (Valerius Maximus 5.2.4) quotes the incident out of context and the other (Frontinus 4.1.13) is more interested in the upshot, which is that the elder Scaurus was so outraged by his son's cowardice that eventually he drove the disgraced young man to commit suicide. We also know from Frontinus that this flight happened at the 'Tridentine Pass' so it would seem logical that Scaurus junior would decide that all was lost when the bridge appeared to be giving way and the fall of the camp on the left bank was imminent. If so, the departure of their cavalry contingent would hardly have helped the morale of the infantry whom they abandoned.

To this we may add another anecdote, this time related by the elder Pliny in his *Natural History*. If we assume that the collapse of the bridge left most of the Romans in the left camp isolated and surrounded by the enemy, then this would be the logical moment for the military tribune who commanded the camp to be paralysed by terror and indecision (as Pliny assures us he was). This proved too much for the leading centurion of the legion, one Cnaeus Petreius of Atina, who attempted to shout some sense into his commander. When this failed, the exasperated Petreius simply killed the man and took personal command of the troops.

After giving the men a comprehensive tongue-lashing, he led them in a ferocious charge that cut through the surrounding enemy and took the troops to safety further down the valley. For this inspired act of mutiny Petreius was awarded the extremely rare honour of the Grass Crown, which was only bestowed upon a man who had saved a Roman army – the only time that such an award was ever given to a centurion. Later, when the armies of Marius and Catulus had united, it was Petreius who was given the honour of performing the celebratory sacrifice. (Pliny *Natural History* 22.6)

It is at this point, incidentally that the version given by Pliny becomes totally incompatible with the version given by Plutarch, who says that the left bank camp was surrounded and attacked by the Cimbri. So far, so much in agreement, but Plutarch then goes on to say that the Cimbri so admired the gallant Roman defence that they allowed the survivors to surrender and depart unharmed. Since a tame surrender, no matter how brave the preceding defence, would hardly grant the leading centurion the unprecedented honour of the *corona graminea*, Pliny's version is to be preferred here, not least because the bestowal of the crown would be a matter of public record. However, this does not preclude the events described by Plutarch from having happened a few days earlier in this campaign, as we have suggested above (p.130).

According to Plutarch, the Battle of Tridentum went directly on from the fall of the camp on the left bank, something which modern historians tend to discount. For a start, if the bridge had gone down, this would have left the Cimbri on one side of the river and Catulus on the other and no way for either side to have resumed hostilities. If the bridge were still intact, holding it against the Cimbri could have been done with about a dozen determined men, as legend says that Horatius had proven in a bygone era. Therefore, we should assume a pause of several days while the Cimbri found their way to the nearest ford (apparently there were several they could choose from once they were downriver) and the gallant Petreius led his men back to the main camp. (Alternatively, if the garrison put up the gallant defence envisaged by Plutarch, this surely must have taken more than the few hours which his description allows.)

The fall of the camp on the left bank is undisputed in our sources, and this begs the question of why the Cimbri did not do as Catulus had feared and simply proceed downriver toward either the Vento or Po valley. They had, after all, taken out the camp on the left bank which was designed to prevent them doing exactly that, so now they had unimpeded passage to the Italian plain of their choice.

It is very probable that there were heated debates among the Cimbric leadership about this very question. Going directly on down to the plain had the advantage of getting the horde on to level ground where the huge number of the Cimbri might allow them to swamp the Romans, rather as they had done at Arausio in Gaul. Furthermore, the mass of humanity which comprised the Cimbric horde liked to eat regularly, and food was more plentiful in the plains than in the high alpine valleys.

On the other hand, the army of Catulus was right there, evidently demoralized and vulnerable. Going on to the plains would not destroy Catulus' legions, but instead give them a chance to pull themselves together once more. Catulus would doubtless follow the Cimbri as they moved deeper into Italy and his smaller force might even be able to get around them and pick a more suitable site for a battle – exactly as Marius was doing with the Teutones. On the other hand, if it proved possible for the Cimbri to take the army of Catulus out of the picture, then when they reached the plains the only possible remaining threat would be the army of Marius. (It would appear that for the moment the Cimbri had completely lost contact with the Teuton branch of their combined attack and had no idea of how their allies were faring.) Certainly, rather than face Rome's last two armies combined, it was better to deal first with the army of Catulus and then – if the Teutones did not do the job for them – with the army of Marius at a later date.

These arguments were convincing enough for the Cimbri to decide to cross the river and close with Catulus for the final part of the Battle of Tridentum. How long it took for all this to happen is unknown as our only direct source for the battle – Plutarch – sweeps us along breathlessly from the attack on the left-hand camp and the bridge straight on to the next phase of the struggle.

It is probable that by the time the Cimbri resumed their assault, Catulus had abandoned his camp on the right bank of the river and was already moving downstream with his army. With the left bank fort fallen there was no point in him remaining where he was. His best chance now was to move down the Adige valley at speed and try to cut off the Cimbri as they struggled across one of the fords which made crossing the river possible downstream from his original camp. Again we have to turn to the scanty material available from Plutarch and note that Plutarch in turn is probably drawing from material which Catulus himself wrote in a natural enough attempt to put his actions in the best possible light.

In fact, Plutarch raises another reason why Catulus might have abandoned his camp and begun to move downstream – if he had stayed where he was then his army would have gone on without him.

Most of the army now showed considerable cowardice, abandoned the camp and began to fall back. Now Catulus, like the excellent commander he was (said Catulus?) showed that he preferred that his own reputation be stained with dishonour rather than that of his country. The terror of his men was so great that there was no way he could persuade them to stay where they were. Therefore he ordered the standards to be taken up, and he himself rushed to the front of the retreating troops. In this manner he made it so that any disgrace would fall upon himself for retreating and that it would appear that his soldiers were not running away but rather that they were following behind their commander. (Plutarch, *Marius* 23)

If we go with this interpretation we can here interpolate an incident described by Frontinus in his *Stratagems* (1.5.3, 'On escaping from difficult situations'). Certainly, Catulus' current situation could legitimately be described as difficult. He was on the right-hand bank of a river with no escape upstream, as we have already determined that the terrain there was too broken to permit passage of an army. Downstream lay the first of the fords which his panicked army would have to use to escape along the left bank of the Adige to safety – except for the far-from-minor point that the Cimbric horde had already crossed over the first of these fords, trapping Catulus and his army on the right-hand bank.

When Catulus arrived and discovered that the enemy held both sides of the river, his next actions seemed reasonable enough to the watching Cimbri. The Romans had arrived relatively late in the day, so Catulus retreated to the slopes of one of the mountains overlooking the ford, there to consider the situation overnight. Roman engineers went about the usual process of establishing a fortified overnight camp and Roman tents started going up to house the legionaries while other soldiers worked at building the standard rampart. Camp workers protected by skirmishers headed into the adjoining forest and began to collect firewood.

Since the arrival of the Roman army, the Cimbri had been stood-to in battle array in case Catulus attempted to rush the ford. Now, since it was clear that there would be no action until the following morning, the Cimbri set about establishing their camp also and scattered across the fields to do some foraging of their own.

Yet the Roman tents visible to the watching Cimbri were the only tents that the Romans had erected. Behind these were not more tents but the Roman army lined up behind their standards with each legionary still carrying his marching pack. As soon as it was clear that the Cimbri had relaxed enough to make impossible an organized defence of the ford Catulus and his army made a determined dash for the river.

Not only did the army get across successfully but Catulus afterwards decided that his opponents remained disorganized enough for him to assay a quick raid upon the Cimbric camp itself. There is mention that a cavalry commander called Opimius distinguished himself on this campaign, and it may have been here that he achieved that distinction by first attacking the camp and then successfully covering the Roman retreat as the outraged Cimbri attempted to take revenge on Catulus' departing legionaries.

While mauling the Cimbric camp was good for the morale of his army, Catulus had to acknowledge that he had now done all that he could in the current phase of the campaign – and what he had done had not amounted to much. In the first instance he had been unable to keep the enemy from crossing into Italy through the high passes. Secondly, he had been unable to hold them in the upper reaches of the Adige valley. Finally, his plan to hold the line near Tridentum had failed, and with the Cimbri now downstream they had multiple crossing points over the river. As Livy's epitomizer had summarized – he was pushed back, and then put to flight.

As things stood now, if Catulus tried to block their route to the plains below, the Cimbri could simply pick another crossing and continue on their way unimpeded. Basically, Catulus had failed in his attempt to keep the enemy from the Italian plain, and indeed he had not even slowed down the enemy advance by very much. On the other hand, even with the advantage of hindsight it is difficult to see what else Catulus could have done. When the enemy had multiple points of entry into Italy he could hardly have blocked every one of them, and in the retreat down the Adige he had at least managed to keep his army intact. If morale had suffered somewhat after the defeat and precipitate retreat at Tridentum, at least the action at the ford had allowed the army to regain some pride. If nothing else, the army of Catulus had now had a good look at the enemy, and several weeks of campaigning had shaken down the troops into a more cohesive army.

It should also be noted that in going into the high Alps to take on the Cimbri, Catulus had been something of an innovator. The usual Roman response to a trans-Alp incursion was to wait for the enemy to finish crossing the Alps and then to take on the invaders in the plains below. For this purpose the Romans had the fortress towns of Aquelia guarding the Veneto, Cremona blocking access beyond the River Po and Milan serving the same function for Cisalpine Gaul. Thus, after the Tridentum campaign, Catulus basically ended up where most Romans commanders would have started. The only difference being that Catulus' army was now

considerably more experienced, and – despite the occasional scare
– still intact.

The downside was that Catulus now had to retreat to Cremona
and allow the Cimbri unfettered access to the Veneto and Po
valley. Twenty thousand Romans were no match for several
hundred thousand opponents on level ground, so the Cimbri had
to be allowed the foothold they had won within Italy. By now
Catulus would be aware that Marius had crushed the Teutones at
Aquae Sextae, and that meant that help was on the way – if only
the complex politicking preoccupying the Senate and voters of
Rome would allow it.

Chapter 10

Towards the Final Clash

O ne might think that having not one but two massive barbarian armies descending from the north, intent on destroying Rome would do a lot towards focusing minds in that city. After all, the last time this had happened was in the fourth century BC when a Gallic horde had descended upon the infant republic, captured Rome and ransomed its citizens. Yet instead, while the existential threat of the barbarian armies certainly contributed to the febrile political atmosphere in Rome, to a large degree within the city it remained politics as usual.

For much of the year the main issue occupying the minds of Romans was not the Cimbric threat but the ongoing feud between Quintus Metellus and Saturninus. Metellus, it will be recalled, was the commander in the war against Jugurtha who had been replaced by Marius after the latter's election to his first consulship. On his return to Rome, Metellus was awarded a triumph for his contribution to Rome's eventual victory and awarded an honorary cognomen, so that he was henceforth known as Quintus Caecilius Metellus Numidicus. To cap off a distinguished career, Metellus was made censor – a magistracy which Rome awarded only to its most venerable politicians.

As censor Metellus ran afoul of Saturninus, who combined the traditional aspect of the job of tribune – making life hard for the senatorial oligarchy – with a penchant for violence and dirty tricks. A generation previously the aristocratic Gracchus brothers had served as tribunes and had tried hard but unsuccessfully to introduce much-needed reforms in Rome. The Gracchi had failed and paid with their lives for their temerity in opposing the senatorial elite, but they were fondly remembered by the common people. Therefore Saturninus knew that he could greatly increase his personal standing if he had on his side a son of one of the Gracchus brothers, a man called Equitius.

The problem was that there was no evidence that Equitius had Gracchan parentage. Indeed, the sister of the Gracchi stepped forward and adamantly denied that Equitius was ever a member of the family, an act that required considerable courage in the face of extensive intimidation by Saturninus and his supporters. Given the lack of evidence for the parentage of Equitius, Metellus the censor refused to enter Equitius as a Gracchan on the census rolls. He went even further and tried to have Saturninus ejected from the Senate due to ethical unfitness to hold his rank. In return, Saturninus raised a mob that attacked Metellus and briefly besieged the censor and his supporters on the capitol. A good number of lives were lost, and in all the uproar the Senate had little time to consider the far more serious events taking place outside the city.

Even as Marius was engaging with the Teutones the slave war raged on in Sicily depriving Rome of much-needed grain and soaking up troops who were desperately needed in the north. Further to the east, another Roman commander was struggling – and failing – to contain a plague of piracy that threatened to bring trade in the eastern Mediterranean to a standstill. And in the midst of all this, the Romans were still mapping out and building new colonies for their citizens in Africa and Asia Minor.

Amid all the politics, wars and rumours of war we find little concern that the Cimbri had now made themselves at home in the Po valley and were comprehensively pillaging the place from end to end. There was a feeling – which Plutarch shares – that military incompetence on the part of Roman commanders had flattered the Cimbri and given the impression that they were more formidable than was in fact the case. Now that Roman legions under Marius' command had a general of the calibre of those men who had defeated Hannibal and conquered the Macedonians, the barbarian threat should be no match for Roman power.

This sentiment was certainly not shared by Marius, the man charged with the actual task of dealing with that threat. He was well aware that even with his and Catulus' armies combined the Roman legions facing the Cimbri made up less than a fifth of the size of the enemy force. While his and Catulus' men were now to a large degree veterans, they were still the only army that Rome had in the field.

If these two armies were overwhelmed, as had been the armies of Caepio and Maximus at Arausio, there would be no saving Rome this time. Marius probably felt that the Cimbri were unlikely to repeat their earlier mistake and turn aside. They would march on Rome and flatten the place, and there would be no time for Rome to recall or raise anything like an army capable of stopping them. So, while Marius was grateful for the trust that the Romans had bestowed upon him, he doubtless wished that by renewing his consulship they did not insouciantly consider that they had basically resolved the issue.

Marius had returned to Rome after his victory. As a newly (re-)elected consul he had essential administrative and religious duties to perform. While in the city Marius was fully entitled to celebrate a triumph for his resounding defeat of the Teutones and Ambrones. Nevertheless, he decided that having a city intact enough in which to celebrate a final victory was more important than an immediate boost to his personal political status – which was about as high as it could get anyway. He therefore eschewed his triumph and instead, as soon as he was able, set out to reinforce Catulus in the northeast. It was essential that he do so, since there remained a clear threat that the Cimbri might decide on an immediate attack southward before the two Roman armies could unite. Therefore, some time around the end of the year 102 BC, Marius caught up with Catulus, who was still holding the line at Cremona. The two armies became a single unit – or, as a pessimist would argue, all Rome's eggs now resided in a single basket.

At this point the war entered a lull. The Cimbri had the Po valley and were in no hurry to leave it after the rigours of their transit of the Alps and the stress of the Tridentum campaign. The Cimbri were not simply a Gallic army intent on the sort of massive smash and grab raid of the sort that Brennus had launched upon Rome several centuries before. The Gauls in the Brennus invasion had been intent on taking their loot home with them, while the Cimbri had come to conquer a new homeland – and the Po Valley and Veneto suited them just fine. The region had after all been only recently conquered by the Romans after being Gallic for centuries. Most of the inhabitants were Gallic and may even have found their new masters more to their liking than the Romans whom they had replaced.

Later historians such as Florus claimed that after Tridentum the reason that the Cimbri did not march on and attempt to attack Rome itself was because life in the lush regions of northeast Italy quickly weakened the bodies and temperament of men accustomed to the harsh northern climate (while not explaining how the Romans even further south avoided being more decadent still). More probably the Cimbri did not press their advantage and march on Rome simply because they saw no reason for it. They had got what they came for, and it was now a matter of defending their gains.

Also, the Cimbri were apparently still convinced that the Teutones were likewise making solid progress on the other side of Italy, and they were waiting patiently for their allies to join them in their new homeland. Although by now some of the survivors of Aquae Sextae had made their way to the Cimbric host with news of the disaster, the Cimbri flatly refused to believe that a force as massive as that commanded by King Teutobad could be wiped off the map in a single engagement. They harshly treated Teuton survivors who insisted otherwise, considering these to be Roman agents spreading disinformational propaganda.

Since Catulus was now unwilling to come north to meet them, the Cimbric leadership may have felt that the Romans had given up hope of reclaiming the Po and Veneto – lands they now considered their own by right of conquest. The only question was how far their new domains would extend, and that, it seemed, was a question to be settled over the course of the next campaigning season.

We have little information of events over the winter, although we can assume that Marius and Catulus kept their troops under arms and spent their time drilling the men until both armies were at the same standard of military readiness. It is possible that it was around this time that two innovations were introduced to the Roman *pilum*. The first of these came about because Marius had noted that the Cimbri had somewhat broad shields – as Plutarch has also noted when describing the Cimbric habit of sliding down mountains on the things. The Cimbric shield was more capable than most at catching a Roman *pilum*, so Marius decided to turn this advantage into a disadvantage.

The Roman *pilum* is different from the average spear in that while the average spearhead is fitted to the end of the shaft, the *pilum* had a very long shank. This shank was made of iron, the quality of which was variable. Possibly this was by design, more probably because the smithies mass-producing the missiles were themselves of variable quality. *Pila* with tempered shanks were better at punching through shields, with an improved chance, therefore, of also punching through the warrior behind it. *Pila* with poor-quality shanks tended to embed themselves into shields and then dangle and droop. Having over six feet of metal and wood stuck in the business side of the shield tended to reduce its utility, often to the point where the user simply discarded it altogether. The Romans were quite keen on this idea because each legionary also carried a second *pilum* which had a devastating effect upon a rank of unshielded warriors.

The iron shank of the *pilum* was secured to the weighted shaft of the spear by two steel pins that prevented the head from separating from the body of the *pilum* after impact. Plutarch tells us that Marius determined that this effect could still be achieved with a single pin, and he therefore ordered that the second pin be replaced by a more fragile one made of wood. This second pin tended to snap on impact, causing the heavier shaft to pivot towards the ground on the remaining pin.

In other words, what bad metal-crafting sometimes performed as a spontaneous droop, Marius had now enabled even well-tempered shanks to achieve, albeit at an angle rather than a natural curve. We need not doubt that this innovation was effective, but modern reconstruction shows that adding the wooden pin is more tricky than Plutarch (who never saw a *pilum* thrown in anger) believed. Rather than an ad hoc alteration done by legionaries on the spot, the new design must have taken a lot of work by skilled craftsmen, and the work was probably carried out over the winter. (cf Christopher Matthew, 'The Battle of Vercellae and the Alteration of the Heavy Javelin (*pilum*) by Gaius Marius – 101 BC,' *Cambridge University Press*: 24 April 2015)

The second innovation was that at least some legionaries inscribed the initials of their commander upon the shafts of their weapons. The reason for this is uncertain, but the probability is that there was a certain degree of rivalry between the two armies. The men of the Marian contingent were naturally cock-a-hoop about their victory against the Ambrones and Teutones. In the manner of military units of all times and places, whenever they met the soldiers of Catulus, Marius' legionaries would have loudly compared their performance at Aquae Sextae with that of the

Catulan forces at Tridentum. An unexpected side-effect of this was to develop an esprit de corps among the Catulan legionaries, who defiantly marked their kit with their commander's name.

It is uncertain and unlikely that either of these developments in *pilum* technology survived the Vercellae campaign. Generally, Roman legions worked under a single commander, so there was no need for soldiers to proclaim their loyalty to their general upon their gear (and indeed no definite examples of *pila* so marked have been found). Also, the chief value of a *pilum* lay in its penetrative power and while Marius was happy to lessen this for tactical purposes under specific circumstances, this was not usually the case. Generally, the Romans wanted more impact, not less, and in later years we see not only better-quality shanks, but also weights attached to the shaft to give the *pilum* that extra heft on impact.

Along with modifications to weaponry, Marius needed to drill the Catulan part of his army in the new formations and tactics which had been so effective at Aquae Sextae. Only when Marius felt that his combined army had been made into an effective enough force did he lead his men across the Po into what the Cimbri now probably considered 'their' territory. A further indication that the Cimbri felt content with their gains south of the Alps is that they did not respond to the Roman incursion with force. Instead, they sent ambassadors to negotiate, hoping that they could end the war on the basis that each side would keep what land it currently held. Therefore, on meeting with Marius, the opening statement of the Cimbri was not a demand for a Roman surrender but simply a re-statement of the fact that they wanted land and settlements of their own, for themselves and their allies, and now that they had that land they were not interested in further fighting.

Rather than reject the Cimbric demands out of hand, Marius decided to use the arrival of the ambassadors for his own propaganda purposes. He was well aware that the Cimbri tended to do their negotiating before a large audience, as they did with all tribal discussions, and he was more than happy to go along with the Cimbric practice on this occasion. Marius knew well how to play to a crowd and he had a strong hand to play. Therefore, he disingenuously asked the Cimbric ambassadors who might be these 'allies' of whom they spoke. The Cimbri replied that they meant the Teutones, at which response the Romans present all burst into laughter. 'Don't concern yourselves with the Teutones', Marius informed the Cimbri. 'They already have all the land they need, bestowed by our hands to be theirs forever.' (Plutarch, *Marius* 24, *passim*)

The Cimbri understood that they were being toyed with and responded with insults and threats, including detailed descriptions of how they would respond to this Roman impertinence once the Teutones joined up with them. Marius affected surprise. 'Didn't you know? The Teutones are already here. Come now and I shall introduce you – it is only fair that you should not depart without a chance to meet your old comrades.' At a signal those captured Teuton leaders whom the Romans had received from the Sequani were produced in their chains, and the sight of these prisoners once and for all shattered the Cimbric illusion that further help would be forthcoming from the west.

In fact, there was never any hope that negotiation with the Cimbric ambassadors would produce a satisfactory peace. There was no way that the Romans were going to accept the loss of territory in the northeast to a barbarian horde, especially as this would land them with numerous, well-armed and predatory neighbours who would only become more of a threat once they had further built up their strength. On the other hand, the Cimbri were certainly prepared to fight for what they now held. They had been wandering all over northern Europe for over a decade and they had now finally found somewhere highly suitable to settle. The Romans would literally have to take it back over their dead bodies, and that was something the Romans were quite prepared to do. Under the circumstances, peace was never an option and Marius had only agreed to talks because that gave him the opportunity to land some psychologically damaging blows upon the enemy.

One question that has never been satisfactorily determined is the whereabouts of the two opposing armies at this point. They were evidently in close proximity for, some time after the highly unsatisfactory meeting between Marius and the Cimbric ambassadors, King Boiorix himself rode out to meet with the Romans. It is clear that by this time Marius had already joined Catulus at Cremona, so the question is what direction he took in his advance into Cimbric-held territory, and how deeply he had penetrated into that territory before he met the Cimbric ambassadors.

It is also fair to assume that, until Marius dashed their hopes, the Cimbri would have been moving westward in expectation that they would eventually meet up with the Teutones coming east. Since Marius had marched into Cimbric territory with the intention of bringing his enemy to battle, he would have naturally moved in the direction of the Cimbric army. His most likely line of advance therefore was up the Roman road known today as the Via Regina to a point somewhere just east of Milan.

Once the Roman and Cimbric armies became aware of each other, there followed the customary dance, with the Cimbri attempting to manoeuvre the Romans on to an open plain where their superior numbers and cavalry could overwhelm the much smaller Roman force. Marius on the other hand was not a general to be forced into a battle he did not want and simply avoided combat while he was still in search of the perfect battlefield. Mostly he stayed quietly in his camp waiting until his scouts found something suitable. This they eventually did, which left Marius with the problem of how to get the Cimbri to fight there.

This problem was helpfully resolved by Boiorix himself. The Cimbri were now aware that the Teutones had been taken out of the war. Disturbing as this was, it probably did not greatly shake the confidence of the Cimbri, who had after all spent much of the past decade massacring every Roman army that they had come across. The problem for Boiorix was that he had a large army spoiling for a fight – a fight he needed to have soon. Once again, as at the start of his campaign against the Teutones, Marius was in a static well-stocked camp while the Cimbric horde was vacuuming up all the foodstuffs available in the area. Simple logistics dictated that eventually there would come a point where the Cimbric horde would have to move on.

This the Cimbri were unwilling to do, because everyone knew that the coming battle would decide the entire Cimbric war. The Cimbri would never be in a better position to finish the Romans off for once and for all. On the other hand, if the Romans were victorious then the Cimbri would not only be driven from Italy, they would probably be finished as a nation. The stakes were about as high as they could get and a decision could not be long delayed.

Since Marius had evidently come north to fight, and the Cimbri were ready, willing and able to oblige, the only question was where and when to have the decisive battle. So Boiorix decided to resolve the issue directly by going to the Roman camp to 'challenge Marius to give him a time and a place where he was prepared to come out [of his camp] to fight for possession of the country'. (Plutarch, *Marius* 25)

Marius responded that he was not in the habit of allowing his enemies to dictate events on his campaigns, but he would make an exception in this case. Since Boiorix had basically given him the challenge of hosting the battle it was up to him to suggest the venue and, fortunately, Marius had the ideal location in mind. He proposed 'the plain of Vercellae', also known as the Raudine Plain, and doubtless pointed out that the width of the plain gave the Cimbri plenty of room to manoeuvre if that was what they had in mind.

The actual whereabouts of the Raudine Plain remains a mystery. Plutarch states that the proposed battlefield was 'three days away' from the Roman camp, because that was the time allotted for both armies to get there. However, since the location of that Roman camp is unknown, this information is not very helpful. One possible site immediately springs to mind, namely that place where the city of Vercelli still stands today. This city is located some 80km (52 miles) west of Milan and could certainly be reached by the Romans in a three-day march. Nevertheless, it is an improbable location for the decisive battle.

Several issues dictate against Vercelli being the site of the Battle of Vercellae. The first is that although a Roman army could get there in three days, this would still count as hard marching even if the Romans started in Milan instead of – as was more likely – from somewhere to the east of that city. The next question would be why Marius was looking for a battlefield so far from his current location, when even somewhat east of Milan would put him at the limit of the lands controlled by the Cimbri. Finally, going west to Vercelli, which is actually in Piedmont, would be directly counter to Marius' major strategic aim, which was to keep his army between the Cimbri and Rome.

The objections to Vercelli as a battleground become even more pronounced when we look at things from the Cimbric point of view. The Romans might be able to manage a march of sixty miles or so in three days, but the Cimbric horde would be hard put to match that pace. We know, because our sources tell us, that the entire tribe were present at the battle including the women and children. The non-combatants would travel by ox-cart, a means of transportation which was a great deal slower than the Marian mule. Overall, the Cimbri would be doing well to get halfway to Vercelli before the designated time for the battle.

Furthermore, at the meeting with Marius, King Boiorix promptly agreed that the 'Raudine Plain at Vercellae' would be a mutually acceptable battleground. The king was certainly not going to take Marius' word for this and march to the location sight unseen. Therefore, he must have already been familiar with the site, which again rules out Vercelli, which is further west than we have any reports of Cimbric territory extending.

In fact, the only reason for choosing Vercelli is the name, and even that is less convincing than it first seems. 'Vercellae' are reeds or rushes in Latin, and the name could have designated any settlement beside a river where the locals gathered the rushes. (These rushes were used in places such as taverns for crude carpeting, and could be woven together to make matting.) As anyone who has been north of modern Milan can testify, the landscape offers an abundance of sites where reeds or rushes could be gathered – indeed the area today is host to an abundance of rice fields. Nor is there a shortage of plains, as the land is reasonably flat right up to the foothills of the Alps.

The 'Raudine Plain' is no help as the name has disappeared from the historical record, and the descriptions given by ancient historians – 'this side of the Alps' (Velleius Paterculus) and 'on a broad plain' (Florus) – do not help to pinpoint the location. Unless archaeology comes up with some useful remnants from the battle (as has been the case where archaeology has succeeded in locating the site of the Teutoberg forest massacre, which happened almost a century after the battle of Vercellae) all that can be safely assumed is that the fateful clash occurred within forty miles of Milan and probably somewhere northeast of that city.

Despite the vagueness of the location, some very specific details about it have survived. For a start, the Raudine plain was at least 30 stadia (6 km) across and it ran from east to west with low hills on the eastern side. The Romans formed up on these hills, so, unless some very complicated manoeuvring took place, this suggests that they approached the battlefield from the west and the Cimbri from the east – all of which agrees with a site somewhere northeast of Milan. There were reeds and a morning mist, which suggests a river, and if this river ran from north to south (as do most rivers in the region, which run from the Alps to tributaries of the Po) then this would have anchored one flank of the Roman army, which would have allowed the Roman cavalry to be concentrated on the other flank, as events during the battle imply that they were.

One difference between the army of Marius and his predecessors seems to have been that Marius appreciated the importance of having good cavalry in large numbers. No commander likes to have his army outflanked, or have large units of horsemen causing havoc around the back of his army. Given the large number of Cimbric cavalry, both eventualities were highly probable without a larger cavalry component than Rome had heretofore fielded. We are given a number of 15,000 for the Cimbric cavalry (by Plutarch) and informed that their preference was to unload javelins at the enemy before charging to finish off their foes with their long, heavy swords. Taking this element of the Cimbric army off the battlefield was one of Marius' priorities and for this he needed a cavalry component capable of at least neutralizing their Cimbric counterparts.

Certainly, the Roman army which marched to the Raudine Plain was not the same sort of Roman army which the Cimbri had been happily massacring over the past decade. Apart from the cavalry, the first, and critical difference was in leadership. While Catulus was no Napoleon, at Tridentum he had played a bad hand about as well as anyone could expect and he had earned and received the trust and loyalty of his soldiers.

Marius was likewise trusted by his soldiers and with even greater reason. If the Aquae Sextae campaign had shown the legionaries anything, it was that Marius was not going to throw their lives away by recklessly engaging in battle. That Marius was an extremely cautious general was nothing but praiseworthy in the eyes of those whose lives depended upon that caution. There was also the undeniable fact that at Aquae Sextae Marius had shown not only that the barbarian invaders could be defeated, but that they could be annihilated, and with relatively minor casualties on the Roman side.

Secondly, there is little doubt that the army had spent the winter being rigorously drilled in the tactics needed to contain the fury of the initial Cimbric attack and the means of grinding the enemy force down thereafter. One advantage of an army largely composed of *caput censi* was that by definition these men had no farms or smallholdings to which they needed to return over the winter and spring. This made them as near to a professional army as the Mediterranean world had seen since the Spartans, and over subsequent centuries the legions were to prove time and again that, all else being equal, well-trained professionals will beat enthusiastic amateurs every time.

In short then, the Roman army that formed up on the Raudine Plain had better generals and better morale, as well as better training, equipment and tactics than the army which had gone down to epic defeat at Arausio almost four years previously. The question which Marius and Catulus must have anxiously asked themselves as the Cimbri slowly filtered on to the battlefield was – would all this be enough?

One factor had not changed. The Romans were still heavily outnumbered. There are only imprecise and conflicting numbers for the two sides but the basics on the Roman side at least are clear. The Roman army had around 50–60,000 men – which is very large for a Roman army, but vastly inferior to the army of 150,000 (Plutarch) or 200,000 (Orosius) men whom the Cimbri brought to the battlefield. The strongest and most experienced part of the Roman army was composed of the veterans of Aquae Sextae, around 30,000 men whom Marius commanded personally. Then came Catulus with around 20,000 men, and finally there was a small unit of around 6,000 men commanded by Cornelius Sulla.

According to Plutarch, Marius divided his part of the force in two, with one contingent on the extreme right of the battlefield and the other on the left. This left the Catulan legions deployed deep at the centre, where Marius clearly hoped that they would play only a minor part in the battle.

There are reasons to disagree with Plutarch when he claims that Marius would divide his troops in this manner. Firstly, splitting his army into smaller components would allow the Cimbri to focus the greater part of their strength on each part of the Roman army in turn and defeat it in detail. Secondly, Marius clearly intended to lead his men in the decisive downhill charge that would defeat one wing of the enemy army and for this he would need as many men as possible – and then some. Attempting to launch an attack with only 15,000 men would be both senseless and suicidal. One way of squaring the circle would be to argue that Marius had placed Sulla under his direct command, and the 'Marian' forces on the extreme right wing were actually those commanded by Sulla.

If this is the case, it is then possible to form a working hypothesis for both how the troops were deployed and Marius' plan for how events would unfold thereafter.

Firstly, as was Marius' wont, he had put the troops on a battlefield of his choosing that played to Roman strengths. As at Aquae Sextae, the enemy would have to advance uphill to get at the Romans, which is a tiring business for men wearing armour and under an understandable amount of stress. If we assume that a river pinned the right flank, there was little chance of the enemy sweeping around that side of the army, so the cavalry could be concentrated on the left, which is where Marius had positioned himself.

Traditionally, the right wing was the place of honour on a battlefield where the best troops were stationed. Therefore, it is legitimate to ask why Marius – who was nothing if not a glory-hound – had yielded this position to Sulla, whom he neither liked nor trusted much. The answer must be that Marius had chosen the left wing precisely because the right was the place of honour and therefore, by positioning himself on the left, Marius expected to meet – and break – the cream of the Cimbric army.

The Marian master plan for the battle then runs something like this. The Cimbri advance on a broad front, with their cavalry trying to get around the Roman left flank but being held back by the unexpectedly strong Roman cavalry contingent. Just before the battle lines meet, Marius sends his men on a furious downhill charge at the Cimbri facing him. This charge pushes the leading Cimbri against those advancing behind, leaving them little room to deploy their long slashing swords.

Meanwhile, the enemy have met Catulus' legions, who break the impetus of the Cimbric charge with heavy javelins and then stand their ground, or at worse, slowly retreat uphill, their right flank covered by Sulla's smaller force. By now, Marius has pushed back the Cimbri facing him, or perhaps even put them to flight, and this allows him to wheel his disciplined troops into the flank of the contingent fighting Catulus. Already confused and demoralized by the sight of their finest troops being defeated by Marius' men, the Cimbri facing Catulus rapidly crumble in the face of this new threat and the entire army starts to disintegrate.

There follows the annihilation of the Cimbric army, adulation in Rome for Marius, and a triumphal parade of the like not seen for a century, in which perhaps Catulus might be permitted a minor role.

This plan was solid enough and it played to the strengths of the Roman army and the weaknesses of the enemy. There were, however, two potentially fatal flaws. The first of these was the assumption that the Cimbri were unsophisticated barbarians and their actions were therefore completely predictable. The other flaw was that, precisely because his plan played to the known strengths and weaknesses of both armies, it was in fact Marius who was being completely predictable. As the battle unfolded it would appear evident that Boiorix and the Cimbric leadership had worked out pretty much what Marius intended to do and had made their own plans accordingly.

Chapter 11

The Battle of Vercellae

Even though it was the end of July, the morning of the
Battle of Vercellae started out with a low fog hanging over
the plain. This may not have been an entirely unexpected
development, for the river from where the reeds which gave
the battlefield its name were gathered would have provided the
necessary moisture. Nevertheless, this must have been an irritant
to the Roman commanders as they led their troops out on to the
battlefield, for it meant that they could not see how the Cimbri
were deploying in the fog. Their own army on the other hand was
completely visible because their deployment on the hillside meant
that the Romans were above the low-lying mist.

This at least can be assumed to have been the case from Florus,
who states that 'prisoners afterwards asserted that because the
Roman battle line was drawn up facing the west, the [morning]
sun reflected the light from the bronze of Roman helmets so that
the sky appeared to be on fire'. (Florus, *Epitome* 1.38.11)

The Cimbri down in the plain began to organize, but even with
a disciplined army such as that of the Romans, getting over one
hundred thousand men into formation takes a while. With the
Cimbri it did not help that the entire nation was there, including
women and children, and these non-combatants formed up their
waggons at the foot of the plain. As was their custom, the women
began covering the bases of some waggons with taut leather sheets.
Once the Cimbri began to move forward, the women would use
these sheets as giant drums, pounding rhythmically upon them in
time with the Cimbric advance.

Said advance was still some time off, because the Cimbri had some complex manoeuvres in mind and the usual protracted process of forming their battle line was further complicated by the necessary extra arrangements. After a while it also became impossible for the Cimbric leaders to head off to sort out trouble spots personally. This was because the best warriors among the Cimbri – who were, by definition, the leaders – had made one of the most bone-headed pacts in the history of warfare. To make sure that no-one backed down or out of the battle line, they had agreed that all in the front rank would be chained together at the waist. While wonderfully macho and heroic, this also meant that the line would be held back by the dead and wounded and that individuals along the line would be completely unable to respond tactically to local events.

While the Cimbri were getting it together (literally, in the case of the chained warriors) the Roman commanders were busy with the sacrifices which preceded any Roman battle. These sacrifices were overseen by the general himself, and usually involved the slaughter of at least one animal so that its liver and other internal organs could be examined to determine the will of the gods in a process called haruspicy. The term 'at least one other animal' is used here because on the verge of battle Roman commanders simply refused to take no for an answer. They had a tendency to keep killing sacrificial victims until the gods finally came up with the right answer. If the gods were feeling peevish the sacrificial altar could begin to resemble a meat-packing plant on a particularly bad day.

To put the gods into a favourable mood, Marius vowed that he would sacrifice a hecatomb of (one hundred) cattle. This was an easy enough offer to make, for Marius probably had at least that number back at the camp as a mobile food reserve. If the Romans won the day, then the army would soon be going home and the food would not be needed. If the Romans lost then very few in the army would ever need to eat again. Either way, this was the end of the long war and the cattle were now surplus to requirements.

Further along the battle line, Catulus was making his own sacrifice. Since he was not in charge of the rations he could not offer foodstuffs to the gods, but instead he vowed to 'consecrate the day'. The meaning of this is uncertain, but the implication is that should the Romans win then Catulus and all his household would thereafter treat the anniversary of the battle with the solemnity of a religious festival, including regular sacrifices and dedicatory prayers.

As the sacrifices were completed and the will of the gods was revealed, Marius cried out with spontaneous surprise, which he had doubtless long rehearsed, 'Oh! Mine is the victory!' (Plutarch, *Marius* 26) The news was quickly taken up by those within earshot (it had probably been a very loud cry) and passed along to those who might have missed it. This helped to hearten the Romans, who could by now through the fog get their first glimpses of the Cimbri, looking like 'a vast sea in motion' according to Plutarch. The background thunder of the Cimbric drums would also have now started rolling across the plain.

The opening move was made by the Cimbric cavalry, who came from the middle of their army, aiming at the Roman left wing in a single massive charge. This would have surprised and nonplussed the Roman commanders facing them. The oncoming horsemen must have been a terrifying sight, for the Cimbric cavalrymen looked particularly formidable upon their large steeds, wearing towering helmets that made their already large bodies appear even more formidable. Yet the more experienced legionaries in the Roman line knew that this display was just that – a display. Horses are in some ways more sensible than humans and few steeds will willingly charge directly into a solid wall of humanity that also has lots of pointy bits sticking out of it. Such cavalry chargers were especially rare in an age before the invention of the stirrup, which enables the rider to stay in the saddle during tricky manoeuvres such as the horse coming to a sudden stop.

Therefore cavalry, as both the Cimbri and the Romans well knew, were basically ineffective against formed infantry, provided that infantry were brave enough to stand in their ranks and stare the enemy down. The Roman line did not break, so, predictably enough, just before they came into contact, the cavalry swerved sharply to their right. The Romans on Marius' flank were then treated to a cavalcade of some 15,000 horsemen galloping across the front between themselves and the advancing Cimbric infantry.

Having performed this dramatic but apparently pointless exercise, the Cimbric horsemen disappeared into their own dust on their right flank, there to engage with the Roman cavalry who were patiently awaiting their arrival. Existing accounts of what happened at Vercellae, vague and contradictory as they are, have come down to us indirectly through the writings of Catulus and Sulla, and neither man was much interested in what happened to the Cimbric horsemen after that first charge. All that is known is that at this point the cavalry gallop off the scene and vanish from history.

However, the cavalry charge affected the battle even after the riders were gone. Firstly, this was because those same Romans who had withstood the charge without flinching reckoned that their steadfastness had forced the enemy into retreat. The shout went up that the enemy were already broken and, despite the best efforts of the commanders, it proved impossible to stop the soldiers from surging forward to follow up their 'victory'. Recognizing the inevitable, Marius was forced to give the signal for the charge that he had anyway intended to order in the near future.

The Roman left wing plunged into the dust cloud left by the horsemen, paused to hurl their *pila* at an enemy they could not see and then drew their swords to advance to contact. The Romans advanced, and advanced, until they were treading upon their own expended *pila*, but the enemy was simply not there. Plutarch's assumption is that somehow the two blocs of a combined hundred or so thousand men missed one another through a complete accident. A better assumption gives some tactical awareness to the Cimbric leadership who could have predicted what Marius intended to do – a prediction made all the more certain once the Roman deployment was visible on the hillside.

If Marius planned to throw his best, battle-hardened troops at the Cimbric right wing then one easy way to take those Roman troops out of the battle would be to side-step the attack, just as a matador side-steps a charging bull. In this case though, instead of a red cape, the Cimbri used the dust thrown up by thousands of horses galloping across the dust of a summer-dried plain.

In other words, for all that not a single Roman was slain by the apparently pointless Cimbric cavalry charge, it had succeeded beautifully. Firstly, the dust cloud had stopped Marius from seeing the Cimbric infantry before him as they wheeled left and merged with the men advancing on Catulus in the centre, and secondly it had forced Marius into a premature charge before the dust could clear. We know from the historian Orosius that there was a brisk breeze that day, and that this came from the east (Florus, *Epitome*, 1.38), so once Marius' Romans had launched their charge they would have been supplying their own dust cloud to supplement the fading residue of the Cimbric cavalry's efforts. Thereafter Plutarch tells us that, lost in the dust cloud, the Marian legions 'shuffled aimlessly up and down the plain for some time' (Plutarch, *Marius* 26).

Marius thus had a frustrating and humiliating battle, for he first had to rally his troops after their futile charge, then await a counterattack which did not come, and thereafter advance cautiously into the choking murk in search of an enemy who was not there. Whether or not the Cimbri had planned it that way – and unlike Roman historians we should give them some credit for military ability since they had already somehow beaten a string of Roman armies – the result was the same. Rome's best general and his best troops had been taken effectively out of the fight. Now it all depended on Catulus and Sulla and their relatively inexperienced troops.

Where previous Roman armies had crumbled before the ferocity of the Cimbric charge, Catulus and his men stood firm. Bewildered Roman historians have offered different reasons for this sudden ability to resist. Plutarch offers the suggestion that the dust was so pervasive that the front-rank legionaries could not see the entire mass of the enemy army as it bore down upon them (despite his earlier comment that from the Roman perspective the Cimbric army looked like a sea of men in motion). By this argument each legionary could see only the man in front of him, and by then he was too accustomed to the sight of Cimbric warriors for the spectacle to greatly dent his morale.

Apparently, Catulus himself asserted that the reason that his men stood firm was because of their superb training which had left them in great physical shape. 'Not a Roman was seen to have broken into a sweat, or to be gasping for breath – and that despite the great heat of the day and the run into combat', Plutarch comments on Catulus' report. (Plutarch, *Marius* 26) Apart from the obvious self-congratulation by Catulus, who as commanding officer was responsible for the training of his troops, this quote gives another important fact, namely that the Catulan legions initiated the encounter with the Cimbri by a short, sharp downhill charge.

It is reasonably certain that the Cimbri who took the brunt of that charge had worked up more than a modicum of sweat. Unlike the Romans who had been resting their elbows on their shields and watching the Cimbri deploy through most of the morning, the Cimbri had been steadily on the move first in forming up, and then in making the slog uphill to where the Roman armies were waiting.

This slog was even longer than usual, for Frontinus (a writer who, unlike Plutarch and his ilk, had actually commanded troops) informs us that Marius had made his camp on the slopes of the hills on the eastern side of the plain and then had simply marched his army out to form up for battle almost beneath the ramparts of that camp (*Stratagems* 2.1.8). Therefore, the Cimbri were forced to advance at least a mile – and probably two – before they engaged with the Romans, and the last part of the advance was uphill. Also, because his legionaries were not going far, Marius had ensured that they were able to get a good breakfast beforehand and start the actual fighting well rested (and sweat-free).

When it comes to the actual fighting, Plutarch has evidently moved on to the account of Sulla, whom he reports as remarking that the barbarians advancing up the hill had other problems also. For a start they had the morning sun in their faces – for apparently a unique quality of Plutarch's dust that prevented the Romans from seeing very far in front of them did nothing to stop the Cimbri from being blinded by the sun to the extent that they had to hold their shields higher to shade their eyes (Plutarch, *Marius* 26.25). The historian Orosius agrees – perhaps from also using Sulla as his source, and adds that the morning mist had also prevented the Cimbri from seeing the initial Roman deployments, despite other accounts of how the Cimbri saw the sun reflected brilliantly off Roman helmets (Orosius, *History* 5.16.14).

So we have the barbarians, blinded by dust and/or the sun, tired from their long march uphill into combat, fighting rested Roman soldiers who had long overcome the initial fear of their large-bodied barbarian foes. Yet for some historians this was not enough reason why the Romans should be victorious. There was also a moral dimension.

The purity of the Cimbric martial vigour, asserted some later historians, had been sapped by their experience of civilization. They had wintered in Venetia where the climate is extremely mild, and the softness of the country had eroded their military prowess, prowess which was already made degenerate after they had encountered bread and cooked meat, not to mention the debilitating pleasures of wine. (Florus 1.38.13)

Florus informs us of this scornfully, while overlooking the fact that the Roman legionaries currently beating up the Cimbri on the hillside were themselves no strangers to cooked food and wine.

Plutarch felt that the reason that the Catulan legionaries prevailed was due to the heat, because the Cimbri raised in the northern cold could not cope with fighting in the heat of an Italian August (or Sextilis as the month was called in Republican times). This would have been a more convincing argument were it not for the fact that Spain gets a lot hotter than northern Italy in summertime, and the Cimbri had spent the past three years campaigning there, apart from another seven years spent in Gaul, Illyria and other parts of southern Europe.

Yet one powerful factor which Plutarch only returns to later was probably more significant. The Marian legions had prevailed magnificently at Aquae Sextae, while the Catulan legions were best known for their ignominious retreat from Tridentum. Unless the character of soldiers, and of human nature in general has changed radically in the past 2,000 years, one can be certain that the Marian legions had pointed out the difference in performance at every available opportunity. The Catulan legions had a point to prove. That same fierce team spirit that had led them to engrave their commander's name on their *pila* meant that they were not going to suffer again the reproaches of the rest of the army if they backed out of a fight. They had a lot of shame and frustration to get out of their systems, and the Cimbri were right there for them to do it.

So, for whatever reason, the Cimbric advance into Italy ended against the wall of the Catulan legions on the slopes of the Raudine Plain. First the Cimbric advance was held and then slowly the barbarian advance was beaten back. Once again, the decision of the Cimbri to chain together their best fighters in the front rank was proven to be an extremely dumb idea. With the Cimbric advance stalled, the Romans were able to pick off the strongest of their enemies at will, for their opponents were chained in place, unable to turn to meet threats or help someone a few places down in the chain gang. And these victims were the cream of the Cimbric army. Once they had felled the enemy's best fighters, for the Romans the rest was literally downhill all the way.

The Cimbric army started to go backwards and it was probably at this point that the Romans managed to land another decisive blow. Plutarch tells us that at some point the Marian legions emerged from their private dust cloud to join in the actual battle, because this contingent of the army later attempted to claim that despite their delayed contribution they had actually done the bulk of the fighting. This claim gains some credibility if the Marian contingent did manage to locate the enemy right at the end of the battle after the Catulan legions had broken the back of the Cimbric resistance.

By hitting the Cimbri on their right flank while they were already going backwards the Marian legions turned a confused retreat into a panicked rout. On an ancient battlefield it was a lot easier to kill an enemy who was desperately trying to escape than it was to defeat an armed man who was competently defending himself. This is why casualties in ancient battles were generally extremely lop-sided, with the victors getting off relatively lightly and the losers being decimated – if they were lucky.

The Cimbri were not so lucky, because the Romans were determined to end the Cimbric threat once and for all. There was the defeat at Arausio to avenge and the Romans were not a very forgiving people. The battle degenerated into a full-scale rout and pursuit in which the Romans ruthlessly chopped down anyone they could reach. Aware that the battle was lost, some of the Cimbric leaders such as King Boiorix grimly determined to go down fighting. Others wanted to make absolutely sure that they would not be taken alive and rushed at each other with drawn swords in a sort of mutual murder pact.

Those Cimbri who opted for safety through flight had another problem. Their tribe's waggons were parked along the bottom of the plain in a long line which made flight difficult. To compound the problem these waggons were filled with Cimbric women who had no illusions about the fate that awaited them should they fall into Roman hands. These women desperately tried to turn their menfolk back to face the Romans – even killing some who refused to turn around – and joined in the combat themselves. The naturalist Pliny the Elder adds that the Cimbric hounds also joined in the battle to defend their homes (*Natural History* 8.61)

So ferocious was the battle at the waggons that the historian Orosius claims that this was as severe as the original conflict upon the hillside. The women, standing on the waggons had the advantage of height, and the reckless courage of those with literally nothing left to lose. The legionaries on the other hand reckoned that they had the battle won and were extremely reluctant to risk life and limb in a conflict which could bring them nothing but dishonour whether they won or lost. As a result, the struggle lasted for some time.

Yet the end was inevitable and in recognition of this the Cimbric women began to kill themselves in large numbers. Many of these made sure that their children died first rather than grow up as Roman slaves. As with their menfolk, some women took turns at killing and then being killed, while others hanged themselves from the waggon posts with hastily contrived nooses. Orosius reports with fascinated horror the incident of one woman who reportedly was hanged when she cut loose the oxen and was pulled into the air by her neck as the waggon pole swung up. She had attached one child to each of her ankles and these were hanged in turn as they dangled from her legs. Lacking convenient trees other women tied their necks to oxen and horses and then goaded the creatures into galloping off.

Orosius also reports that the Romans scalped the female corpses. This he alleges was done to demoralize those still fighting but there was probably an ulterior motive also. Roman women were fond of wigs made of blonde hair (cf Martial, *Epigrams* 6.12) and if deprived of the booty of living humans, the legionaries were not above looting the merchantable parts of their bodies.

In the end Plutarch reckoned that some 60,000 women were captured, yet twice that number had preferred death. As to the men, no-one was in the mood to wander the plain counting corpses and in any case the numbers were far too great for any such attempt to succeed. By most accounts the Romans lost less than 1,000 men, which sounds trivial until one realizes that this still accounted for one in every 50 Romans who fought that day. Nevertheless, the Roman casualties pale in comparison to those suffered by the Cimbri.

Of the men in the massive host that took the field in the morning, almost all finished as corpses or prisoners by sundown. Estimates of total Cimbric casualties range from 100,000 killed or captured (Velleius Paterculus, who probably was only counting combatants) to 160,000 killed and a further 60,000 captured (Livy, who included the civilians). Essentially then, whatever the actual death toll, the migrant nation of the Cimbri died on the Raudine Plain.

Chapter 12

Aftermath

It is interesting to speculate what might have happened had the Cimbri won the battle of Vercellae. The first thing to note however, is that the Cimbri did not even come close. If we are to believe that the cavalry manoeuvre was designed to send Marius charging aimlessly into the dust, then this says that the Cimbri had a plan when they went into the battle and they executed it perfectly. It wasn't enough.

Even if the chain of events which led to the fruitless charge of the Marian legions was due only to happenstance, the result was the same – Rome's best soldiers and the nation's best commander were taken out of the picture for the crucial part of the battle. Yet even with everything working in their favour, and the cream of the Cimbric nation pitted against the relatively inferior troops of Catulus, the result was a massacre. The Cimbri were killed on a scale which made the casualties from previous Roman defeats – epic as these were – seem minor by comparison.

In other words then, up to Vercellae the Cimbri had been fortunate. They had seen Rome's legions only at their worst, poorly commanded and caught out of position time and time again. At Vercellae the Cimbri ran into well-commanded, well-positioned, well-trained troops with good morale and those troops chopped them to pieces.

Even though he was absent from the battle for the actual fighting, the fingerprints of Marius are all over the victory at Vercellae, and he rightly was awarded a Roman triumph for his actions. For a start, the Roman legionaries who defeated the

Cimbri were a different breed from the men who had died at Arausio just half a decade earlier. They were better trained and and believed in themselves, and for that Marius was responsible.

Secondly, for all that Marius himself was pulled out of position, his decision to position his army on the eastern slopes of the battlefield and let the enemy come all the way across the plain to him was doubtless one of the decisive factors in the Roman victory. As the Battle of Aquae Sextae shows, this was a very deliberate choice arising from careful deliberation as to the best way to blunt the initial ferocity of the Cimbric charge.

Indeed, when we read the accounts of Tacitus and Cassius Dio of the so-called Battle of Watling Street in Britain over 150 years later, we see such close similarities that it seems that Marius' tactics against the Cimbri had become standard Roman military doctrine. At Watling Street, again we see Roman troops divided into three groups, waiting for the enemy (in this case the rebels of Boudicca) to cross the battlefield to launch an uphill charge, and again we see the Romans making a short downhill counter-charge before the lines came into contact. Again, the enemy broke and fled, only to be trapped against the waggons containing their womenfolk.

In short, once Marius had deployed his troops at Vercellae the scene was set for something close to an inevitable Roman victory. But what if Marius had not been in command? What if the snake-pit of Roman politics had caused Marius to be deposed and replaced by a senatorial donkey with the malign incompetence of a Servilius Caepio or Papirius Carbo? What if Marius had succumbed to a bout of food poisoning in Africa, or died of appendicitis, and instead of a well-trained and precisely-deployed army at Vercellae, disorganized and demoralized Roman troops were caught out of position on an open plain somewhere around Milan and overwhelmed?

Had they won against the Romans in 101 BC, would the Cimbri have realized that the Italian peninsula was not big enough for themselves and the Roman Republic? Had the Cimbri decided that Venetia and the Po valley were enough and settled down to defend their gains, there is little doubt that the Romans would eventually have gathered their strength, found a competent commander and reconquered northern Italy – no matter how many tries it took. The Romans were like that.

On the other hand, if the Cimbri had observed that a victory in northern Italy had taken out the only army between themselves and Rome and then decided to march on the capital things would have become very interesting. It must be remembered that at this time the Roman Republic was in a somewhat delicate condition, as the slave rebellions in Sicily and Campania had demonstrated. Furthermore, Rome's Italian subjects were so disaffected with Roman rule that a major civil war was just a decade away – and indeed it is arguable that only the threat from the Cimbri prevented that war from breaking out before the end of the second century BC.

Had Rome fallen to the Cimbri after a victory in North Italy, then Rome's reluctant subjects might have hastened to make peace with the victors if given guarantees of their own security – guarantees that the Cimbri would have given cheerfully. Their own territorial ambitions were limited to northern Italy and they would have had as little interest in occupying Samnite or Lucanian country as did the Langobards of six hundred years later (who were content to occupy what later became Lombardy). Even if one does not subscribe to the 'great man' theory of history, it seems that without Marius, Rome's nascent empire might have crumbled before ever it got properly started.

The danger facing Rome from the Cimbric invasion was therefore very real and the significance of Marius' victory at Vercellae should not be underestimated. Indeed, even in defeat the Cimbri significantly affected the course of Roman history.

The first way that they did this was in the effect that the Cimbri had upon the character of Marius. Without the Cimbric Wars,

Marius would have been seen by later historians and contemporary Romans as a competent commander who had brought to an end the Jugurthine War by successfully building upon the groundwork laid by his predecessor Metellus Numidicus. Since Marius was a poor politician, his return to Rome after the African war would have been followed by a return to civilian life after which he would have been quickly elbowed out of public life and forgotten.

Instead, because of his victories in north Italy, Marius was seen as a second Romulus, the saviour to whom Rome owed its continued existence. And this was not just how Marius was seen in the public eye – from his subsequent career it is evident that this is also how Marius saw himself. Given this self-image as a sort of military superhero, it becomes more understandable that Marius' first concern after his magnificent win at Vercellae was to disguise the relatively ignominious role that he himself had played in the actual battle. The undeniable fact was that while the victory was largely due to his training and deployment of the army, the battle itself was actually won by the Catulan legions.

So, the first thing that Marius did after the battle was to deny that fact. This was hard to do, because it was the soldiers of Catulus who had taken the Cimbric camp and all the Cimbric battle standards, treasures and symbols of power were now in the possession of Catulus himself. Catulus had also captured several of the Cimbric leaders and – much to his personal satisfaction – the same golden bull from the Tridentum campaign upon which defeated Romans had been forced to swear that they would no longer fight against the Cimbri (p.130). This bull thereafter became a treasured possession which Catulus kept in his house as an enduring proof of his role in the Roman victory.

Nevertheless, Catulus was merely a proconsul while Marius was consul and the actual commander of the joint army. Marius was legitimately entitled to take control of the actual plunder, and there was a lot of this. The Cimbri had looted their way down through Germany and across Gaul and Spain, and as an itinerant people, they had kept most of their treasure right with them in their waggons. This plunder now belonged to Marius and the soldiers whom he commanded. The only question was how much Catulus and his legionaries were entitled to share.

Given that the Catulan legions had done the actual fighting, they could reasonably be expected to expect a large share but we have seen that Marius had his own reasons for wanting to downplay their role and the role of their commander. For a while the disagreement threatened to become serious, for there was considerable rivalry between the Catulan and Marian legions. Plutarch (*Marius* 27) confirms that if that rivalry did not previously exist – and it almost certainly did – it definitely existed now.

In the end it was decided that the matter should be settled by a panel of arbitrators from the city of Parma. If modern Vercelli were indeed the site of the battle, it seems rather odd that these arbitrators should be drawn from a city over 200km away. However, this might be explained if these Parmesians were a diplomatic embassy from that city calling upon the Roman consul (Marius) on non-military business.

One can imagine the sentiments of the diplomats who had come to engage with the consul in bloodless discussions as they instead picked their way across the gore-soaked battlefield while hardened military experts explained why the swollen corpses lay where they did, and the manoeuvres which had resulted in them being in those positions. Finally, and probably with considerable reluctance, the men of Parma decided that the evidence against Marius' claims was too clear to be gainsaid. To a large degree this was because the Catulan legions had inscribed the name of their commander upon their *pila*. These *pila* were now sticking out of Cimbric corpses while Marian *pila* still lay in the dust into which they had been ineffectually discharged. The conclusion could only be that Catulus was entitled to share in the triumph and he and his legions were entitled to a considerable share of the loot.

The commentator Valerius Maximus later remarked, 'The site of Flaccus' house, after it had long remained unbuilt, was finally adorned by Q. Catulus with the spoils of the Cimbri.' (Valerius Maximus, *Factorum et Dictorum Memorabilium* 6.3.1) That is to say, by way of emphatically claiming his share in the victory at Vercellae, Catulus built there the Catulan Portico with part of the loot allocated to him from the battle. He used much of the rest of his share on a temple which he built to celebrate 'The Fortune of that Day' [on which the Cimbri were defeated]. After his setbacks at Tridentum, Catulus was determined that his abilities as a general should be publicly recognized. He later went on to play a distinguished role in defeating the rebellion of Rome's disaffected allies in 90 BC.

Ever the politician, once Marius realized that there was no denying the role of Catulus and his legions at Vercellae, he pretended to welcome this conclusion. Nevertheless, things got tense again when Marius came to celebrate his victory in Rome. Marius used his great fame in an attempt to sideline the Catulan legions. He did this so unsubtly that the Catulan soldiers got the impression that they were to be dropped from the proceedings of the triumph altogether. Fortunately, the Senate stepped in when they realized the dangers of unfairly depriving Catulus' men of honours fairly won – especially when those men were a large, well-armed army parked right outside the gates of Rome. In the end Catulus, Marius and both their armies together shared the well-deserved triumph.

Marius' true feelings about his loss of face became clear only much later when he took control of Rome during the civil war of 87 BC. Catulus was prosecuted by a close relative of Marius, though on what grounds is uncertain, mainly because everyone knew the real charge was 'making Marius look bad at and after the battle of Vercellae'. Realizing that condemnation and execution were inevitable, Catulus locked himself in a newly-plastered room and there lit a charcoal fire knowing that the combined effect of the fumes would lead him to a painless death. By that time Marius and Catulus' former subordinate Sulla were already mortal enemies – something which also had adversely affected Catulus' chances of survival.

One reason for Marius' bitterness was that by the time he instigated the death of Catulus, Marius was well aware that his own career had reached its zenith at Vercellae and had been on a downward trajectory ever since. Immediately after the battle, Marius had spontaneously granted Roman citizenship to two cohorts of Camertine troops who had withstood the brunt of the Cimbric charge. This was blatantly illegal, and when reproached with the fact Marius insouciantly replied that 'the din of battle had drowned out the murmur of civilian laws.' Such was his surging popularity at the time that he got away with it.

Yet, thereafter, the poor political skills of Marius let him down. He was re-elected consul yet again but was unable to contend with the powerful influence of the Roman aristocrats who remembered his cavalier treatment and the many (and well-deserved) insults which Marius had thrown their way in the past. Marius retaliated by joining forces with the demagogic Saturninus, and his reputation fell when that politician also fell.

Then came the long-expected war with the Italian allies, a war which brought a new crop of military heroes. Much to Marius' chagrin, these included his former subordinate Sulla. Marius' own performance as a commander in that war could be most kindly described as mediocre, and it seemed that thereafter the 'saviour of Rome' was doomed to fade away while resting on the laurels of a victory most people had already forgotten.

Yet having tasted the adulation of the Roman people once, Marius was determined to somehow recreate the glory of his victories in the Cimbric Wars. He made a desperate attempt to get command of a war in Asia Minor and when that failed he resorted to political chicanery to get command of the army transferred to himself from the general to whom the Senate had given the job. That general was Sulla, and Sulla did not take kindly to being removed from his position. Instead, he marched his army on Rome and so began the first of the debilitating civil wars which eventually led to the ruin of the Roman Republic.

While the Cimbric wars and Marius' desperate attempts to hold on to the glory that these wars had gained for him became yet another skein in the pattern of politics of Rome's collapsing Republic, what of the Cimbri themselves?

While many Cimbri chose death on the battlefield rather than slavery, tens of thousands of Cimbric men and women were captured. Most of these were sold locally to work as farm slaves in the very lands of the Veneto which they had once proudly claimed as their own. (Doubtless the Cimbric occupation had led to a degree of depopulation and a consequent labour shortage.)

The Cimbri may have turned up again in the Third Servile War of 73–71 BC, which is better known today as the 'revolt' of Spartacus and his gladiators. In this uprising Spartacus gathered into his army large numbers of freed and escaped slaves, and it is known from Plutarch that many of these recruits were 'Germans'. It is highly probable that some of these were either the offspring of captured Cimbri and Ambrones, or, given that the rebellion happened some thirty years later, possibly grizzled veterans of Vercellae and Aquae Sextae taking one final opportunity to declaw the Roman wolf. If so, the last of the prisoner Cimbri either died when Spartacus' army was finally crushed or this segment of the nation merged thereafter with the servile population of Italy and lost their identity.

Not all the Cimbri were killed or captured in the massacre at Vercellae. Many others escaped from the battlefield and some were never at Vercellae in the first place. Thus, while that climactic battle shattered the Cimbri as a nation, some fragments lived on inside and outside Italy. Julius Caesar came across one such fragment in 57 BC in the course of his conquest of Gaul. He describes the meeting in his own words.

> The Aduatuci...carried all their possessions into one town that was abundantly fortified by nature. .... They [The Aduatuci] were descendants of the Cimbri and Teutones. When they were marching into our province [i.e. Transalpine Gaul] and into Italy these people left behind on the far banks of the Rhine such items in their baggage train that they could not easily bring with them. (*Gallic War* 2.29)

It must be remembered that the Teutones envisaged some hard fighting ahead. Some of their more bulky items of booty would at this point be little more than encumbrances for an army that already could not move very fast. The Cimbri had even more incentive to leave many of their goods behind. Their nation was looking to loop about the northern side of the Alps, through rugged terrain and hostile territory before descending into Italy via the alpine passes at the start of winter. The lighter they could travel, the better.

> They left 6,000 men as a guard to defend their baggage. After the destruction of their fellow-countrymen these guards had to withstand the attacks of their Gallic neighbours. Over the years they went from defending themselves to waging war offensively, and then back to the defensive again. Eventually a common peace was agreed upon and the Aduatuci chose this town as the place where they would settle. (Ibid.)

This splinter of the invasion force had evidently done well for themselves, for by the time Caesar caught up with them they could muster 19,000 warriors. One of the reasons the tribesmen resisted Caesar was because they feared that if they surrendered they would be disarmed and left to the mercy of neighbours who would immediately attack and destroy them. Sadly, these warriors were as powerless against well-generalled Roman troops as their predecessors had been at Aquae Sextae and Vercellae. Caesar killed some 4,000 of them, then captured the town and transported the inhabitants in chains back to Rome, where they were sold as slaves.

Caesar then went on to campaign against a formidable Gallic tribe called the Nervii. Caesar does not describe this tribe as Cimbric, though the later historian Appian called them 'descendants of the Cimbri and Teutones' (Appian Ep 4.) It is more probable, though, that some of the Cimbri who did not go to Spain joined the Teutones who went north into Gaul. These peoples eventually settled among the Nervii and merged with them in later generations. (That the Cimbric remnants chose to live in Gaul rather than Germania, and that they were allowed to do so, is perhaps another indication that the Cimbri were indeed a Celtic rather than a Germanic people.) It is perhaps significant that one settlement in the territory of the Nervii is now known as Kimbri in the local dialect. Today it is better known to the world in general as Cambrai – a lively little city, and the site of a major battle in the First World War.

There has also for years been a debate on the question of whether some of the Cimbri who escaped from Vercellae did not return home to Jutland but instead took shelter in the isolated alpine valleys of north Italy. It is alleged that some remnants of the shattered nation have survived in such locations into the modern era. Thus for example the inhabitants of parts of the Veneto, such as Asiago, have long claimed that their ancestors were members of the Cimbri. This is a matter of some local controversy, because others have claimed that these ancestors arrived – as did the ancestors of many modern Italians – at the time of the barbarian invasions at the end of the Roman Empire, or even during the medieval period.

As with many such controversies, it was hoped that genetic studies might provide at least a partial answer. Tests have shown that these 'Cimbric' descendants have some genetic markers which suggest Celtic origins. However, the alleged descendants of the Cimbri in Italy have no close genetic connection with the alleged descendants of the Cimbri in their original home in Jutland. Therefore, the main centre of 'Cimbric' settlement in Italy remains today more famous for its Asiago cheese than barbarian remnants. There has also been speculation that tribes in Bavaria and even the later Jutish invaders of Britain might have had Cimbric origins, but again these claims are controversial and disputed.

The discussion therefore moves on to the Cimbri of Jutland, where there certainly were surviving Cimbri. This was partly because not everyone set out on the great adventure to southern Europe and partly because a few survivors of the catastrophe eventually struggled back to their former homeland. Again, Appian is helpful here as he confirms that 'although they were now greatly weakened and for that reason rejected by everyone, some Cimbri returned home, having inflicted and received many injuries in the course of that journey (Appian, *Illyrian Wars* 1.4). The continued existence of the Jutland Cimbri is clearly stated in the records of the early Roman Empire because at that point the Cimbri again came into contact with Rome. In his *Res Gestae* (section 26) the Emperor Augustus reports:

I sent a fleet which travelled from the mouth of the Rhine [north]eastwards from the mouth of the Rhine. This fleet reached the lands of the Cimbri, and until its arrival there no Roman had ever come so far either by land or by sea. The Cimbri … and the Germanic tribes of that region sent ambassadors seeking the friendship of myself and of the Roman people.

The geographer Strabo enlarges upon that meeting, and claims that the Cimbri offered their apologies for their misbehaviour of a century previously. In his *Geography* (7.2.1), Strabo tells us that the Cimbri 'still occupy the lands which they held in earlier times'. A (later?) delegation from these ancestral lands came to Augustus transporting with its members 'the most sacred kettle in their country'. This 'kettle' is probably one of the cauldrons reported from earlier times as being used to capture the blood of prisoners as their throats were slit. Why the Cimbri felt that Augustus would like so blood-stained a gift is uncertain. However, this does show that the Jutland Cimbri still retained Celtic rather than Germanic customs, and did so a century after much of the population had left their homeland never to return. As it happened, Augustus accepted both cauldron and apology, after which the Cimbric ambassadors sailed off, though thereafter their people still pop up occasionally in the historical record.

Archaeology may be able to fill some of the other gaps. For example, in Borremose in Himmerland an ancient fortress town recognized as Cimbric has been excavated by modern archaeologists. This place was occupied for a period estimated at approximately 300–100 BC. At the end of this period the place was suddenly and briefly abandoned before being resettled a decade or two later. There is a layer of sand over the peat at this location which is contemporaneous with the start of the Cimbric migration. One reading of this evidence is that the Cimbri abandoned the area after the disaster from the tsunami which drove so much of the population from their homes. Later resettlement happened either after some Cimbri returned to their former homeland, or after the non-travelling Cimbric population expanded enough for some formerly deserted villages to be re-occupied.

It is also worth noting that after this point Roman-era artefacts began popping up in Jutland in burials and peat bogs. These may have arrived in Jutland through trade or have been directly imported by those returning from Italy either at the time of the invasion or later. Of particular interest is a Roman military dagger, which supports epigraphical evidence that some Cimbri may have served with the Romans as volunteer auxiliary soldiers.

Pliny the Elder, writing some eight decades after Vercellae, felt that the Cimbri had become strong enough to be counted as part of one of the major confederations of Germania, and in this he was possibly drawing upon the work of one Pomponius Mela, who wrote a little-known *Geographica* a generation previously.

Perhaps the last word on the survival of the Jutland Cimbri should go to a contemporary of Pliny, the historian Tacitus.

In a distant part of Germania live the Cimbri, at the edge of Ocean. [The great sea which the Romans believed circled the world]. They are now an insignificant tribe, but one of considerable fame. There remain many signs of how great they were in their glory days – including the remnants of their massive camps on both sides of the Rhine. From the circuit of their perimeter it is clear even today what military power that tribe possessed, and one can see there evidence of their massive migration. (Tacitus, *Germania* 37)

It would appear that in the end the Cimbri suffered the same fate as the Roman Empire. In the migration period which saw the end of imperial Rome, it was not only the lands around the Mediterranean which were forever changed by the mass movement of barbarian peoples. At some time in the sixth century the Cimbric heartlands in Jutland were occupied by the

Jutes, and thereafter evidence of the independent existence of the Cimbric peoples slips away. It is one of the small ironies of history that the tribe which once threatened to destroy Rome in its mass migration was in turn wiped out by another migrating people.

Index

INDEX OF ANCIENT AUTHORS AND TEXTS